Oak Island Secrets

Revised Edition

Mark Finnan

Formac Publishing
Halifax, Nova Scotia
1997

Formac Publishing acknowledges the support of the Canada Council and the Nova Scotia Department of Education in the development of writing and publishing in Canada.

Canadian Cataloguing in Publication Data

Finnan, Mark

    Oak Island secrets
    Rev. Ed.

ISBN 0-88780-414-4

1.Oak Island treasure site (N.S.). I. Title

F1039.025F56 1997	971.6'23	C97-950092-3
FC2345.024 F56 1997		

Formac Publishing Company Limited
5502 Atlantic Street
Halifax, Nova Scotia
B3H 1G4

Printed in Canada

Distributed in the United States by:
Formac Distributing Limited
121 Mount Vernon Street
Boston, Massachusetts 02108

Dedicated to
Deirdre, Aengus, Tanya and Laura

Contents

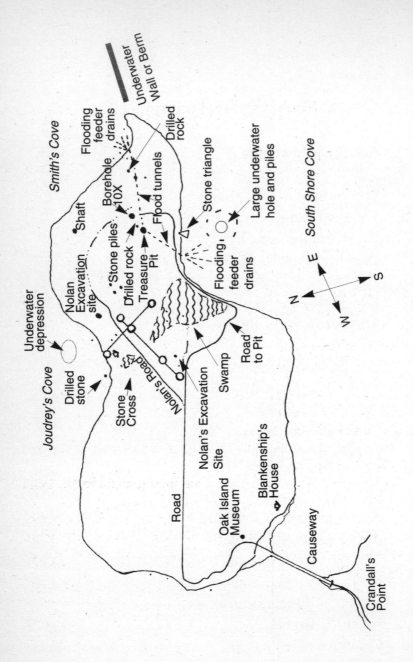

Locations of discoveries, work areas and stone markers.

Acknowledgements

I am grateful to the many people who helped me in the course of writing this book. I wish to thank current treasure hunters Dan Blankenship, Fred Nolan and David Tobias for sharing some of their time and information about their work on Oak Island with me. I am especially thankful to Mr. Nolan for allowing me free access to his property on several occasions.

I am indebted to Major Gerald G. Vickers, past Grand Secretary of the Grand Lodge of Nova Scotia A.F. and A.M., for his most helpful cooperation, and also to past Grand Master Frank E. Milne. I am also grateful to the staff at the Public Archives of Nova Scotia, the Special Collections section of the Killam Library at Dalhousie University, the Nova Scotia Museum of Natural History, the Lunenburg Public Library and the Halifax Herald Ltd. in Halifax.

I wish to thank others who provided me with helpful material: Jim and Helen Adams, David and Nancy Cameron, Doug Denesha, Norman Glen, Elizabeth Green, Bill Gilkerson, George McClean, and Martin and Elizabeth Sovie.

I have appreciated the many considerations shown by Ken and Nancy Petrie of the Oak Island Inn.

For her generosity and interest, I am most grateful to Dr. Petra Mudie, and I also thank Charles Crowell for his help.

I would like to thank Carolyn MacGregor and James Lorimer of Formac Publishing for their initial interest and subsequent support, and to thank my editor, Douglas Beall, for his excellent work in editing the manuscript.

Finally, I wish to acknowledge wholeheartedly the infinitely valuable assistance and support provided by Helène Thibert.

Maine Boats and Harbours

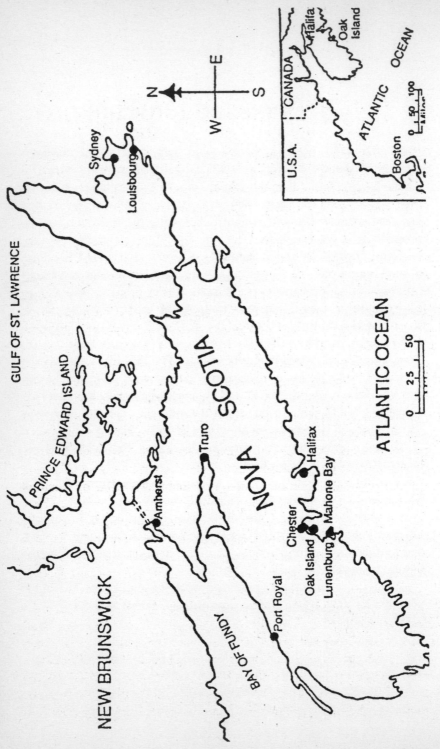

GULF OF ST. LAWRENCE

Sydney

Louisbourg

PRINCE EDWARD ISLAND

NEW BRUNSWICK

Amherst

Truro

NOVA SCOTIA

Halifax

Chester

Mahone Bay

Oak Island

Lunenburg

Port Royal

BAY OF FUNDY

ATLANTIC OCEAN

0   25   50

N
W   E
S

CANADA

U.S.A.

Halifax

Oak Island

ATLANTIC

OCEAN

Boston

0 50 100
Miles

1

My Journey to Oak Island

When I announced to friends I was staying with in Norfolk, Virginia, that I was heading for Nova Scotia to work on the second draft of a film script a Toronto production company had expressed interest in, theatre director Edward Fitzgerald humorously remarked that I should check into the story about a mysterious treasure believed to be buried on a small island up off the east coast of Canada. He said one of the theories was that the treasure might contain the long-lost original manuscripts of the Shakespearean plays. The matter seemed quite remote and improbable to me at the time as I sat enjoying lunch and overlooking the wide expanse of Chesapeake Bay. Because Fitzgerald knew neither the name nor location of the supposed treasure island, the conversation passed on to something else.

Family matters delayed me in Ontario for another month or so, but shortly after arriving on the south shore of Nova Scotia in late October 1992, I discovered, much to my surprise, that I was living close to the site of one of the world's great unsolved mysteries and one of the longest treasure hunts in history. By what seemed to be a remarkable coincidence, Oak Island was in fact only minutes away by water from the porch of the secluded shoreline cottage I rented for the winter. I was soon intrigued and captivated by various aspects of the Oak Island mystery, so much so that I decided to look into it myself. Having learned that the treasure had not yet been found, I also vaguely hoped that I might get lucky and come across a clue or two that could help solve the two-hundred-year-old enigma. At the very least, I hoped to satisfy my own curiosity and produce an in-depth and timely article on the subject in the process.

The more I learned about the mystery, the more surprised I became that I had not previously heard about it even though I had worked as a journalist and news announcer in Canada for more than eight years. My ignorance was all the more amazing when I discovered that the various articles and books written about Oak Island and the treasure hunt had been the subject of several television programs, including a much-repeated episode of "Unsolved Mysteries." It seemed like I was the only person in Canada, or at least in Nova Scotia, who had never heard about it. Had it not been for a casual remark made by a friend during lunch some two thousand miles to the south, I might never have taken an interest in this remarkable story.

After arriving in Halifax without prearranged accommodations and checking into a harbourside motel, I had set out to explore the city before getting down to the business of finding a suitable place to live. Halifax offers an attractive mix of tangible early Canadian history, especially in some of its public buildings and older homes. Since my script had an early Irish/Canadian background, I was pleased to discover the city has several universities with libraries I could use and a lively cultural scene with a strong Celtic flavour. There was even an eclectic and convenient mix of small restaurants in what otherwise looked like a decaying downtown area. Although I was sure to find a place to live and work within several attractive residential areas with tree-lined streets, I woke one morning savouring the sight and sound of the sea and decided to find a cottage on Nova Scotia's attractive south shore.

About thirty minutes south of the city on Highway 103, the exit sign for the village of Chester caught my eye. Remembering that I had met someone from there at a conference in the United States some time earlier, I pulled off the highway. A quick check in my address book and a call from a garage phone booth confirmed that my acquaintance was in and pleased to have me stop by. While driving to her house outside Chester, I found myself overlooking the broad vista of islands, sea and shore that is Mahone Bay. The attractive panoramic view, reminiscent of several I had enjoyed in my native Ireland, connected me to the locality as if caught up in a deja-vu experience.

I was pleasantly surprised to discover from my contact, soon after I arrived at her house on Borgel's Point, that a fully furnished and equipped waterside cottage was available for rent nearby. Situated well off the road, surrounded by pine and birch and a pleasant view of the bay, it was an ideal location. The next day I unpacked, rearranged one end of the living room as my office space and got to work on the script.

A few days later I received a phone call from my nearest neighbour, Hazel Stos, a pleasant, chatty retired school counsellor, who invited me to morning coffee with a few of the other folk in the area. Although reluctant to leave my work, I went along. After the usual introductions and chit-chat about the weather, the conversation got around to me and my purpose for being there. I obliged with a few background details and a brief description of the project I was working on. On hearing that I was a writer, one neighbour blithely suggested that I should also write about the famous Oak Island during my stay. At that moment I had absolutely no idea what she was talking about, so I said very little in response. Perhaps sensing my uncertainty about the subject, Hazel drew aside the curtains on the kitchen window and pointed to one of several islands out across the bay. "That," she told me, pointing to the largest in sight, "is the famous Oak Island." Others in the room joined in a chorus of comments about the treasure believed to be buried there and recited a litany of various theories associated with its nature and origin.

Suddenly it dawned on me that this was the mysterious island I had heard about in Virginia. My curiosity was naturally aroused, as much by the coincidental circumstances as by Oak Island itself. Over a second cup of coffee, I asked question after question about the treasure search, which I was surprised to learn was still ongoing. One of those present in the Stos kitchen that morning happened to be Robin LeSueur, a retired librarian from Harvard University. Being a book collector with a lively interest in the history of the area, he had amassed a small collection of literature on the subject which he kindly offered to loan me. I found myself returning to my cottage with an armful of material about Oak Island and its elusive treasure.

Determined to stick to my script-writing schedule, I put the Oak Island literature to one side and returned to my desk. However, sometime that afternoon, while taking a breather from the challenge of writing authentic Irish dialogue, I casually picked up one of the books. It was *The Big Dig* by D'Arcy O'Connor. The publisher's blurb on the back cover said this was the most recent publication about the Oak Island mystery, described as the longest, costliest and most hazardous treasure hunt in history. I flipped through the pages, stopping to read whenever a chapter title or paragraph caught my eye. A statement by Mendel Peterson, former Curator of Historic Archaeology at the Smithsonian Institution in Washington, D.C., held my attention. Peterson, who had been associated through his professional position with various other treasure hunts, was quoted as saying, "Oak Island is one of the most fascinating archaeological sites in the New World dating after the arrival of the Europeans. It could possibly have great historical significance." There was obviously some substance to this extraordinary story of a mysterious buried treasure.

I read on and was further amazed to discover that a business syndicate had in recent years been attempting to raise $10 million to dig the largest and deepest shaft ever put down on the island. This eighty-five-foot-wide, steel-encased shaft was to be sunk some two hundred feet into the ground, below bedrock, to reach and extract the treasure. Wooden chests believed to contain at least part of the treasure had been drilled into one hundred feet below the surface in 1849. Unfortunately they had fallen further underground and evaded successive treasure hunters for nearly 150 years. Ingeniously devised water traps had prevented anyone from getting their hands on the elusive treasure.

Further reading revealed that millions of dollars had already been spent in futile attempts to find the treasure, and six lives had been lost. However, more recently, images of chests had appeared on film shot in a water-filled bedrock cavern some 230 feet into the ground. Efforts to reach them had almost resulted in a seventh death, which according to local prophecy shall occur before the treasure search finally ends. I also learned that two separate and at times mutually hostile treasure hunts had been under way on the island for the past thirty years. Oak Island was obviously not for the weekend treasure hunter, the underfinanced or the faint-hearted.

Later that day I picked up an article which outlined the various theories concerning the nature and origin of the treasure. It seems that just about every missing treasure known to man could have ended up on Oak Island. Since the discovery of the deep man-made Pit on the island's southeast end in 1795, a wild range of possibilities had emerged. Some early treasure hunters had expected to find the ill-gotten booty of the famous pirate and privateer Captain William Kidd. Others were convinced the treasure contained gold and other valuables removed from South America by the Spanish conqueror Francisco Pizarro. There were theories involving Inca and Mayan treasures, Norse settlers, and Native miners, as well as theories connecting early English and French colonization activities with Oak Island. Several even speculated that the treasure had a religious origin; these included everything from the Holy Grail to the missing ecclesiastical treasures of pre-Cromwellian England and involved everyone from the Middle Eastern Coptic Christians of the first century A.D. to idealistically minded Elizabethan adventurers.

As interesting as all these were, I was more fascinated by the fact that there was a theory, and a substantial one at that, associating the Elizabethan genius Sir Francis Bacon and the missing original Shakespearean manuscripts with Oak Island. After reading that in 1804 a large and unusual stone slab with cryptic writing on it had been found in the Pit ninety feet below the surface, and that in 1897 a tiny piece of parchment with writing on it had been extracted from what appeared to be a large concrete vault buried much further down, it was obvious to me that something far more valuable than pirate plunder still lies buried on Oak Island. Appreciating how providence had led me directly to this amazing story, one that I felt more people should know about, I settled down to read one of the books from cover to cover. It was early the next morning before I finally put it down.

The checkered history of the two-hundred-year treasure search and the descriptions of the extraordinary discoveries made on the island made compelling reading. The fact that prominent public figures—including a president of the United States, a president of the Toronto Stock Exchange and a trustee of the Royal Ontario Museum—had been involved over the years lent an air of credibility to the claims by other participants, many of them successful businessmen and engineers, that a remarkable treasure lay buried on the island. These claims were, however, for the most part speculative and based on the extensive man-made workings found on and below the surface of the island over two centuries.

At the same time there was hard scientific confirmation of the age and nature of some of the unusual things found in the treasure pit and elsewhere on the island. Coconut fibre and wood taken from tunnels below bedrock were ascertained to be hundreds of years old. There were hand-wrought nails, pieces of a very old ship and sea chest, parts of an ancient wooden slipway, hieroglyphically inscribed stones and several stone markers. There was even a hand-worked stone shaped like a human heart. Evidence of an elaborate underground flooding system and an intricate web of tunnels under part of the island seemed indisputable. Clearly something of an extraordinary nature likely involving a treasure of some significance had taken place on the island hundreds of years before. I put down the book thinking that if only ten per cent of what I had read was remotely true, then the whole story deserved checking into and writing about.

Excited by the prospect of doing research on this well-guarded secret, and pleased at finding myself living so close to the island, I eventually fell asleep. But sleep did not come easily that night, especially because the mysterious island lay no more than minutes away over the calm, moonlit waters of Mahone Bay.

I woke early the next morning vividly remembering a simple but exhilarating dream. Having studied holistic dream work, and familiar with the instructive dynamic in many dreams, I placed my attention on it. The central figure in the dream was a friendly girl of about ten dressed in white. She happily introduced herself to me as the daughter of the manager of one of the early projects on the island and mentioned him by name. Taking me by the hand, she had eagerly escorted me onto the island and shown me a specific location where she said treasure lay buried. In the dream I felt completely trusting of this child and grateful she had shown me where the treasure was. This had all taken place in daylight on what had seemed to be a warm summer day. I had no problem recalling the details of the dream and immediately wrote it down, making sure to fully describe the location pointed out to me by the girl.

While heating water for morning coffee, I began to wonder if the dream was merely an unconscious wish fulfilment based on my enthusiasm over some of the information I had digested the night before. But I also could not dismiss the possibility that the dream had other interpretations, including a literal one. After all, there have been many well-documented instances of clairvoyant dreams, and I had previously experienced several related to my work.

After cranking up the heat to dispel the damp and chilly morning air, I searched among the bedclothes for the book I had been reading the night before. Scanning through its pages, I failed to find either a picture or detailed description of the spot I had visited in my dream. I began to question whether the location pointed out to me actually existed on the island. While finishing my coffee and enjoying a spectacularly fiery sunrise over the waters of the bay, I flipped through the several articles and books about Oak Island loaned by the retired librarian. Some had enlarged overhead photographs of the island, and in a few of these I could clearly see the area shown me by the girl. I came to feel the distinct possibility that the dream had a direct and literal meaning after all.

This dream had left me more anxious than ever to visit the island. I donned the warmest clothes I could find and settled for a distant view from the front porch. The rising sun was burning away a flimsy mist from the waters of the bay as I climbed to higher ground nearby. I stood on the crest enjoying the vibrant glow of the day's young light across the wide expanse of sky, sea and shore that is Mahone Bay. As the thin blanket of mist was dispelled from the waters below, I was given a clear lengthwise view of Oak Island. I sat down on a log to gaze at the mysterious island, the surrounding waters and the horizon beyond.

The damp morning air, the urge to have some breakfast and the need to get back to work put an end to my early morning daydreaming. After all, my script was the reason I was there in the first place. I had a job to do and a living to earn. With limited time and finances, a son and daughter at university and a hot film script waiting to be finished, I could ill afford to idle away precious hours fantasizing about buried treasure. However, as I returned to the house, I decided I would try to visit the island sometime later that day.

During a mid-morning break from my writing, I picked up the second book I would read about Oak Island. It was written by Reginald V. Harris, the lawyer and associate of several of the principals involved with Oak Island during the first half of the twentieth century. I discovered he was considered the official historian of the treasure hunt, at least up to the late 1960s. His book, with the simple title *The Oak Island Mystery*, had become the bible for later writers and researchers, of which there have been many. Harris's description of the early days of the treasure hunt was more detailed, if less stylishly written, than the others, and the book provided me with an unexpected insight into an important aspect of the mystery. Harris certainly had impressive credentials. Not only had he been a prominent Nova Scotia lawyer and a noted judicial and church historian, he had also been a thirty-third-degree Mason and the Past Grand Sovereign of the Grand Lodge of Nova Scotia. According to the jacket notes, this factor might have a bearing on the mystery of Oak Island.

I was already aware that Freemasonry and its secretive rituals had been transferred to the fledgling colonies in North America from Europe during the seventeenth century. I was also aware that its largely beneficial influence had spread into various avenues of the religious, political and economic life of the continent in later years. I was thus intrigued but not surprised by the suggestion that the organization may be somehow connected to the mystery.

Masonry, according to several recent bestsellers on the subject, has been associated with just about every progressive development or treacherous conspiracy in the history of the world, depending on whom you believe. This fraternity and the associated sixteenth-century esoteric spiritual movement known as Rosicrucianism had aspired to some of the highest ideals known to man and sought to preserve and perpetuate these truths in private and public affairs. Many of the teachings of Masonry, if not its secret initiation practices, had of late become more widely understood by many individuals outside the Order. Anyone with a spiritual perspective on life and an understanding of Jungian psychology would have little trouble interpreting Masonic ritual and symbolism.

My work as a writer and researcher had provided me with a reasonable knowledge of ancient religious practices and the use of universal symbols in dreams, legends and iconography. Despite the inaccessibility of source materials, contradictory stories about its origins and controversy surrounding its history, there is little about Freemasonry and its symbols that is not meaningful and understandable. Its possible part in the Oak Island mystery was an unexpected surprise, but one that I felt would make my research all the more worthwhile. I had not come to Nova Scotia expecting to find something so compellingly interesting. I certainly had no intention of digging for the treasure myself; in any case, from what I had read so far, many more experienced and better financed individuals than myself were probably already in line ahead of me.

The possible Masonic connection also interested me in light of the theory associating Sir Francis Bacon with the mystery. Knowing that Bacon was considered a powerful influence on the evolution of seventeenth-century Freemasonry and Rosicrucianism in England and their transferences to the New World, I began to give serious consideration to the possibility that Oak Island had been used as a secret repository of spiritually and historically important treasures. Among these could be the missing original Shakespearean manuscripts, as the plays themselves were not only profoundly philosophical but had been associated with Bacon and the "Rosicrucian Enlightenment" by many serious researchers on the subject.

I returned to my writing more convinced than ever that a well organized and financed group of individuals had carried out the burial on Oak Island hundreds of years earlier. Because such great pains had been taken to hide and protect the treasure, I concluded that the treasure had been meant to be retrieved only many years later by others who could understand the coded messages left in stone. I also felt strongly that the treasure needed to be brought to the surface, assuming that was still possible, so the true nature of the Oak Island mystery could be finally revealed. Naturally, I was anxious to know more about the activities and plans of the current treasure hunters: the Oak Island Exploration Company of Montreal and Frederick Nolan of Bedford, Nova Scotia.

After several hours of making scene changes in the script, I stopped for lunch. I took the opportunity to phone Dan Blankenship, the Oak Island Exploration Company's field manager on the island, to arrange an interview with him. A woman who identified herself as his wife answered the phone and informed me that her husband was not available and she did not know when he would be, period. My journalistic instinct was too strong to be affected by this put-off and I was still determined to visit the island later that afternoon. During lunch I picked up one of the articles I had borrowed. Written sometime in the early 1980s, it began with a brief description of the history of the Oak Island treasure search. Half way through the article the author described an interview he had had with the Blankenships about the early days of their involvement with the mystery.

Dan, it turned out, had been a successful building contractor in Florida before becoming involved with the treasure search as the result of reading about it in a *Reader's Digest* article. He had at first invested money in another individual's operation on the island, but in 1975, after committing himself full-time to the project, he had built a bungalow on the island and moved there with his wife and three children. The article was a nice human-interest piece, but what made it most interesting to me was a statement by Jane Blankenship, made during a conversation between her husband and the writer, that she had had a psychic experience about the treasure while travelling to Oak Island from Florida. She explained to the somewhat bemuddled interviewer that she had been shown that Dan would find something related to the Virgin Mary on Oak Island. By way of establishing credibility, Dan Blankenship had then begun to talk about Edgar Cayce, the famous American psychic, and the fact that many people have precognitive experiences from time to time.

Having done research into the psychic material provided by Edgar Cayce and written several articles about the man and his work, I was greatly tempted to call the Blankenship house again to discuss the matter further. However, the tone of the response to my earlier call had not been very encouraging. Assuming I had simply phoned at an inconvenient time, I decided to let it be and hoped to raise the subject during a later conversation. I put the article down on the table, thinking that my visit to Nova Scotia was getting more synchronistically interesting by the hour.

By mid-afternoon I had quit work and was driving out along the bumpy private road leading from my shoreline cottage to the old coastal highway. After following it along the water's edge to the village of Western Shore, I carefully negotiated the twisting curves of the Crandall's Point road to the causeway leading onto the island. Along the way I thought of the statement made by Mendel Peterson of the Smithsonian Institution that Oak Island was a fascinating archaeological site that could have great historical significance. I thought of the involvement of men such as Franklin D. Roosevelt and Reginald Harris, both high-ranking members of the Masonic fraternity, and of the remarkable and unusual discoveries that had been made on the island. I thought of the dramatic dream or vision experienced by Jane Blankenship, who had spent the last twenty years on the island, and I recalled my own starkly simple but exhilarating dream and wondered again what it could mean. I was hoping I would get to see the location pointed out to me by the girl, and I began to think about what I would actually do if I found some trace of the buried treasure.

Entertaining this exciting possibility, I almost failed to notice the heavy metal chain strung across the mainland entrance to the causeway. I quickly brought my car to a stop in front of a sign which told me the island was privately owned and closed to visitors. It would be several months before I would actually get to visit the island, and then only because of the persistence of a British television crew.

2

The First European Settlers

Oak Island is the largest island in the inner reaches of Mahone Bay, the widest bay on the southern shore of Nova Scotia. Measuring no more than a mile long by half a mile wide, the island's peanut shape gives it two expansive central coves. A third large cove is found at its eastern tip and several smaller ones indent its shoreline. The island, one of more than three hundred in the bay, lies at a northeast to southwest orientation close to the shoreline, not far from the estuary of the Gold River and some smaller streams. With its higher, softly rounded eastern extremity covered by majestic red oaks and its low-lying central marsh cradled between two inviting coves, it must have presented an appealing landfall to those who decided to use it to conceal treasure. Being the only island with a stand of oak trees had made it stand out to European sailors sailing into the bay from the beginning. An account of the inner reaches of Mahone Bay given by Nicholas Denys, an associate of Isaac de Razilly, the French nobleman who established a settlement at nearby LaHave in 1632, makes reference to the oak trees and is the first known description of the area. And some of the Nova Scotia red oaks that grew on the island were used in the burial of the treasure.

According to a Halifax-based geologist I consulted on the matter, Dr. Petra Mudie, its drumlin-shaped contours and hardwood forestation could have indicated to a naturalist aboard an approaching ship in earlier times that the island contained deep, digable soil atop a predominately limestone bedrock. Her written report to me on the geological nature of the Mahone Bay area and Oak Island in particular also indicated that the lower shoreline of earlier centuries might also have exposed the cavernous nature of the limestone foundation. This feature would have convinced an experienced eye that Oak Island offered suitable conditions for the deep and secure burial of a valuable treasure.

A geological survey carried out by the Canadian Department of Mines in 1929 established that the eastern end of the island is formed of limestone, gypsum and sandstone, while the wider western half is composed of quartzite and slate. The soil is made up of a deep layer of hard, bluish clay mixed with boulders of glacial origin. Dr. Mudie pointed out that the different bedrock formations intersected by a central, low-lying swamp area may indicate that the island was actually two smaller ones in the distant past. The rising waters of the North Atlantic have been steadily encroaching on the island at the rate of at least a foot every one hundred years, and recently there has been more rapid erosion on its southern shore, perhaps in part due to the construction of a causeway in 1965. The fact that several items hundreds of years old were found deeply buried under sand and shore suggest that some evidence of the work related to the burial of the treasure has long since disappeared below the rising water level and the eroding shoreline.

First surveyed by Charles Morris back in 1762 and divided into thirty-two lots of four acres each, the island was given the less attractive name of "Gloucester Isle" by cartographer J.F.K. DesBarres in his circa 1779 map of what he called "Mecklenburgh Bay." This attempted name change did not stick and the island, which has also been called "Smith Island," reverted to its former and more appropriate identity.

Following a few sporadic and unsuccessful attempts in the second half of the sixteenth century, the first known European settlement of any consequence in Nova Scotia came about because of the interest of Henri IV of France. In 1604 Pierre de Gua, Sieur de Monts, a Huguenot merchant from Saintonge, was granted a colonization charter by the king, given a ten-year monopoly of the fur trade on the North American continent between latitudes 40 and 49 degrees and appointed vice-admiral and lieutenant-governor of an area to be called New France. He was joined in this adventurous enterprise by explorer and geographer Samuel Champlain; the enterprising aristocrat Jean de Biencourt de Poutrincourt; and Parisian lawyer and writer Marc Lescarbot. Along with more than a hundred artisans, craftsmen, soldiers and clerics, they established an attractive self-contained settlement at Port-Royal on the northwest coast of the province on the Bay of Fundy in 1605, after a disastrous attempt the previous year across the bay on Isle Sainte-Croix, in what is now Maine.

The "Habitation" had a precarious eight-year existence under the influence of court intrigue at home, Jesuit conniving for control of the colony and insufficient funding. In 1607 Champlain left with De Monts to found Quebec, and in 1614 the Habitation was abandoned by a weary Poutrincourt after being attacked and partially destroyed by Samuel Argall and a band of English mercenaries. However, some Frenchmen remained and set up a trading post in the region. The local discovery in 1827 of a large stone with the Masonic square and compass and the date 1606 carved into it has led to speculation that Port-Royal was the site of one of the first unofficial Masonic lodges in North America.

A century later, following the intermittent exchange of control of the territory between England and France—which saw an English settlement under Sir William Alexander take temporary root close to the Habitation and saw Isaac de Razilly establish a French settlement on the South Shore at LaHave—a meagre and poorly supported English garrison had been founded in the sheltered surroundings of Port-Royal, whose name had been changed to Annapolis Royal. However, a massive French garrison was positioned at the opposite end of the province on the exposed and bleak coastline at Louisbourg and a mushrooming French-speaking Acadian population lived in between. Following the Treaty of Utrecht in 1713, France ceded to England her prior claim to "all Nova Scotia or Acadia according to its ancient boundaries" but retained the islands of Cape Breton and St.-Jean, later renamed Prince Edward Island. Colonel Richard Philipps was appointed British governor of Nova Scotia in 1717, a post he held for the most part in absentia, until Colonel Edward Cornwallis arrived on the scene in 1749.

An interesting consequence of Philipps' appointment was that his nephew Erasmus James Philipps, who visited the province with him on two occasions, later established the first official Masonic lodge in Nova Scotia at Annapolis Royal in 1738. From then on, Freemasonry, which had members from the monarchy, the military and the public service within its ranks, played a prominent part in the development of the political and social life of the province. Philipps had likely been introduced to Masonry while on government business in Boston, where Henry Price had been appointed Grand Master of the Masons of Massachusetts in 1733, the same year the Grand Lodge of St. John's in Boston had been warranted.

Functioning under the authority of the Grand Lodge of England, which had been founded in London in 1717, these individuals and lodges fostered the spread of Masonry in Nova Scotia and New England. Erasmus Philipps, as provincial Grand Master, authorized the creation of the first lodge in Halifax in 1750, which had none other than the newly appointed Governor Edward Cornwallis as its Master. Cornwallis had come from a family which had had a lengthy and continuous association with English Masonry. His nephew, Charles Cornwallis, who was to surrender to the prominent American Mason George Washington at Yorktown in 1781, was also a member of the Fraternity.

In 1745 the New England settlers under Governor Shirley of Massachusetts, considering themselves vulnerable to the entrenched French military presence on Cape Breton and tired of repeated raids by French privateers, mounted a successful attack on Louisbourg. The victorious New Englanders celebrated by riotously enjoying the prizes of conquest, but their elation over their victory and new-found security turned to disgust three years later when England handed Louisbourg back to France in the Treaty of Aix-la-Chapelle. This move led to deep distrust of British authority among many of the colonists and is considered to have been an influencing factor in their later decision to declare independence. It also caused the persistent Shirley to demand that an English fortress be built on the south coast of Nova Scotia to deal with any future French aggression. The ideal site was the wide inlet in the centre of its southern shore which the native Mi'kmaq called Chebucto, "the big harbour." Shirley also suggested to his masters in London that they set up a permanent settlement of loyal, hardworking Protestant stock to counterbalance the Catholic Acadian population already present in the province.

These suggestions were favourably received in London, and the Lords of Trade and Plantations drew up a plan for their implementation. The government gave its consent, and under the direction of the board's president, Lord Halifax, recruitment for the Nova Scotia settlement began in March 1749. The hoped-for response from skilled tradesmen, seasoned farmers and retired soldiers did not materialize, however. When the well-equipped expedition sailed down the Thames the following May, many of the ships' decks were filled with London's downtrodden and deprived. That the expedition succeeded as well as it did was in no small measure thanks to the sensible advice offered by Shirley and his staff in Boston and the diligent and comprehensive preparations carried out by the Board of Trade. No expense had been spared in providing all the provisions and essential personnel needed for the initial construction and survival of the settlement. Medical staff and equipment were dispatched alongside engineers, surveyors and masons. Pumps were installed on the ships to improve sanitary conditions and provide some comfort for those below decks. Providence also played a part in the venture by providing Edward Cornwallis as the expedition's commander-in-chief. A temperate and educated aristocrat, he was also an able and experienced soldier and administrator, even at the age of thirty-six. His presence and abilities unquestionably added to the success of the operation.

After only four weeks at sea, Cornwallis's ship sighted the Nova Scotia coastline. Following a brief stop off Merliguesh, the future site of Lunenburg, the party sailed into Chebucto harbour, the future site of Halifax, on June 21st. The other ships, carrying more than 2,500 passengers, arrived soon afterwards, reporting the loss of only one life, a child's, during the crossing. Given the numbers and the dangers involved, this was truly an amazing accomplishment. In his early dispatches back to London, Cornwallis gave a glowing account of the terrain, vegetation and fishing. He was much less complimentary regarding the work habits of some of his fellow countrymen, many of whom were happy to enjoy the free provisions but reluctant to dig and cut their way through the inhospitable landscape or do any other work for that matter. A few weeks later the new arrivals were visited by Major Paul Mascarene, the deputy British governor stationed at Annapolis Royal, on the other side of the province. On July 14th, Governor Cornwallis presided over the first government council, gathered around a large table in the cabin of one of the transport ships in the harbour.

Preliminary fortifications and primitive dwellings were quickly built, but within six months more than a thousand men, women and children had lost their lives to typhoid fever, the bone-chilling cold and Mi'kmaq raiding parties being compensated by the French. However, the determined Cornwallis and his advisers were not deterred from fulfilling their mission, and by the following summer the town was taking shape in earnest. Streets had been laid out and serious construction was under way. Lumber arrived from Boston for the first church, and before long the attractive edifice of St. Paul's Anglican Church, replicating a design by English architect James Gibbs, rose out of the wilderness.

Cornwallis, supported by several members of his command, also made it his business to petition Erasmus Philipps of Annapolis, the Grand Master of Freemasonry in Nova Scotia, to issue a warrant

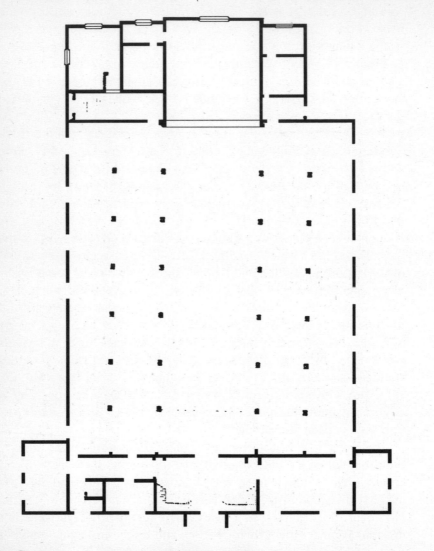

St. Paul's Anglican Church, Halifax, 1750.
The original interior space consisted of a nave and two aisles. The two additional aisles were added in 1868 and the sacristy a few years later. Not only the original rectangular space, but also the present space and the length of the choir contain 318" in their dimensions, as well as the windows and the columns. 318 has long been regarded as the mystical number for Jesus Christ.

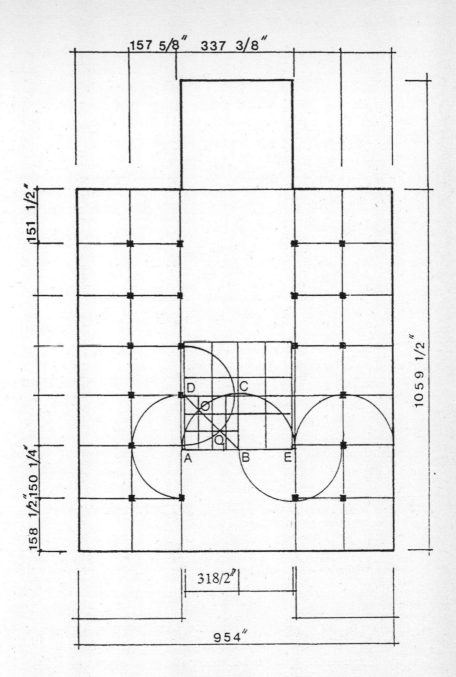

Geometry of the Interior Space, St. Paul's Anglican Church, Halifax

establishing a Masonic lodge in Halifax. This was a natural development, as there already was a tradition of field, or travelling, lodges among English regiments going back several years; Cornwallis had been part of that milieu, which was to include other notable Nova Scotian military commanders such as Jeffrey Amherst and James Wolfe. The warrant was promptly and duly issued, and with Cornwallis as Master, the lodge held its first colourful ceremony at St. Paul's, which, as Professor Atilla Arpat demonstrated in his detailed article in the fall 1994 edition of the *Nova Scotia Historical Review*, was built according to Masonic principles of sacred Christian architecture.

Halifax grew rapidly to become the unchallenged military stronghold and commercial capital of the developing province, often referred to by the more settled New Englanders as "Nova Scarcity." Many of the impoverished Londoners attracted to Nova Scotia by the promise of free land and a year's supply of provisions had proven to be unsuitable for the arduous work of clearing and settling a new land and were unenthusiastic about carrying out the orders of the military command. Blackflies, primitive living conditions, bitter winters and the constant fear of attack by the French and Mi'kmaq did little to endear them to their new home. The despairing Cornwallis, encouraged by the more experienced Governor Shirley of Massachusetts, petitioned the Board of Trade in London for more suitable immigrants. This request resulted in the settlement of more than a thousand German-speaking people in the area that became known as Lunenburg. King George II of England had family ties with the principalities of Brunswick and Lunenburg in Germany, and many of these settlers came from that region.

During the second year, essential supplies continued to arrive from the old country and New England and the settlement gradually took root. Sturdy wharves were built to accommodate the supply ships and trading vessels, and enterprising entrepreneurs arrived and set up various business ventures. Redcoats and rangers patrolled the perimeters of the expanding town, and blockhouses were built to ward off hostile intruders from the interior. Strategically positioned cannon placements along the shoreline guarded the entrance to the harbour from French naval attack.

The influx of these German-speaking immigrants led to the creation of an area in Halifax later called Dutch (Deutsche) Village and to the construction of the simple little Dutch Church, the predecessor of the more elaborate and circular St. George's, which, according to Professor Arpat, also contains elements of sacred Masonic architecture. With the growth of a more stable population and commercial expansion came some of the earmarks of increased social civility. In 1752, Canada's first newspaper, the *Halifax Gazette*, made its appearance. Published by John Bushell, it was printed on a press brought to Nova Scotia from Boston. Cornwallis returned home to England wearied by the challenges and tribulations of the gargantuan task he had accomplished. Governorship of the province passed over Colonel Thomas Hopson, who authorized the transfer of hundreds of German-speaking immigrants southward past Mahone Bay to Merliguesh under the diligent supervision of Major Charles Lawrence in June 1753. The location offered at least one good natural harbour, several bays and, most importantly, good agricultural land. Surveyor-general Charles Morris had been busy laying out lots, which were eagerly taken up and improved by the no-nonsense, self-sufficient settlers. Anxious to put their own stamp on their new home, they changed the name to Lunenburg. As unintentional as it may have been, this change created additional historical Masonic links to the area, because the principalities of Brunswick and Lunenburg had been major Masonic centres in Europe.

In 1755, following the demise of a large French fleet on its way to Louisbourg, the British authorities made a militarily expedient decision to expel the Acadian population from Nova Scotia. This human tragedy, so much lamented in story and song ever since, might have been avoided had less biased minds and more trusting hearts prevailed. The action caused untold hardship to a whole population and left a scar on English and French relations in British North America that would fester for many years. Nor did the expulsion bring the conflict to an end. One year later, the Seven Years War broke out in Europe and extended to the colonies. By the time it was over, France's hold on Canada had been broken, with the final surrender of Louisbourg and the defeat of the French forces under General Montcalm in Quebec on the Plains of Abraham.

In 1757 a petition to the Masonic Grand Lodge in London signed by Governor Charles Lawrence and others resulted in the establishment of the Grand Lodge of Nova Scotia in 1758, the same year the colony elected its first Assembly. The political system was slowly changing towards the more democratic forms already in existence in the colonies to the south. Under the direction of the British Board of

Map of Nova Scotia 1755. Public Archives, Canada.

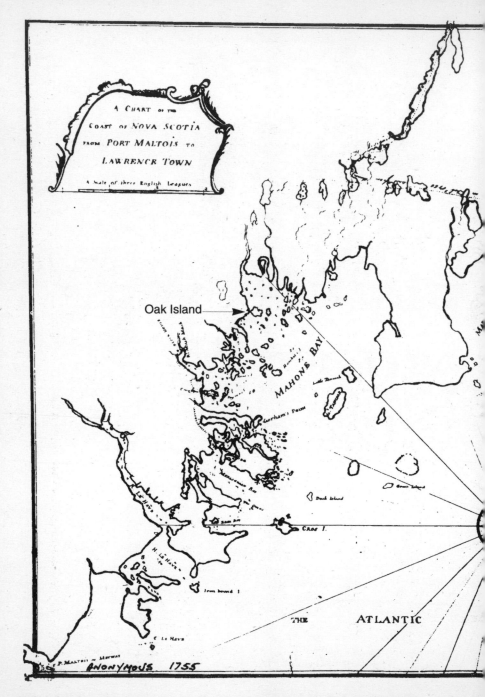

Oak Island is the largest island closest to the shoreline of Mahone Bay.

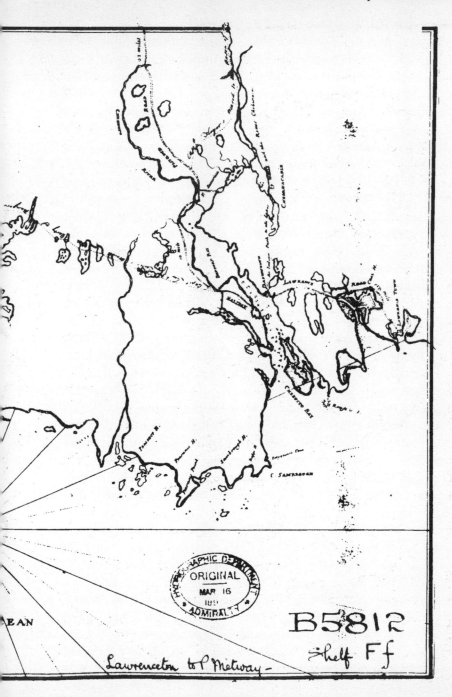

Lawrenceton to P. Metway

Anonymous, 1755

Trade in London, Lawrence issued a proclamation, repeated in 1759, and published in the Boston *Gazette*, inviting colonists from New England to settle in Nova Scotia. New England fishermen were already familiar with the coastline of Nova Scotia, and the province was in many ways a seasonal home to them. Prospective settlers were offered sizable land grants which were rent-free for the first ten years. Freedom of religious worship was guaranteed to all Protestants, and those willing to settle in the northern colony were assured that the form of government in Nova Scotia would be the same as in New England, with a representative Assembly. In addition, each township was to have its own fortifications, manned by British troops. Oak Island was part of the Shoreham grant of some 100,000 acres offered to settlers from New England, who came from places such as New York, Boston, Concord, Lexington and Casco Bay. The earliest European settlers in the Oak Island area had actually arrived after the founding of Halifax in the mid-eighteenth century; now the second batch arrived in 1759 at the inlet where the township of Shoreham, now Chester, was established.

The American Revolution of 1776 was prompted to a large degree by the imposition of the Stamp Act of 1765 and other measures advantageous to British treasury and trading interests. The so-called American rebels had the sympathy, if not the wholehearted support, of many Nova Scotians who, having family and commercial ties with the other colonies, also felt disenfranchised and put upon by the decisions of a mainly military administration and the tax-grabbing tactics of a far-flung empire. The empathy in Nova Scotia was such that some public figures made statements openly agreeing with those to the south who expressed opposition to unfair taxes.

Several in Halifax paid a price for playing a role in the rising tax revolt. One of these was Anthony Henry, who took over from John Bushell as publisher of the colony's first newspaper, the *Gazette*. In 1765, following the example of Master Mason Benjamin Franklin, the inventive publisher of America's first newspaper, the *Pennsylvania Journal*, Henry had brought out an issue of the *Gazette* framed in black that mourned the pending demise of the publication "from a disorder called the Stamp Act." Henry even had the courage to use unstamped paper, thereby depriving the Crown of revenue while opposing the law created to collect it. This bold political statement cost him his position and his paper.

One of Chester's first leading citizens was the liberty-minded and industrious Captain Timothy Houghton, the village's first moderator and sawmill owner, who actually tried to get the locals to join the American Revolution. In spite of his standing in the community, this act of political temerity within the shadow of Halifax also cost him dearly. He lost much of his Chester holdings and later died in Halifax of smallpox after being confined to jail.

Another prominent early Chester settler who supported the American Revolution was the Reverend John Seccombe, a dissenting clergyman from Boston whose ministry had led to the building of the first church in Chester. His pulpit pronouncements in favour of the rebels landed him in court and cost him five hundred English pounds. However, he remained with his ministry until his death in 1792. Chester's loyal reputation was redeemed by Dr. Jonathan Prescott, a former army surgeon and surveyor, who imaginatively deployed local women to defend the village from American naval privateers.

The self-serving actions of these free-wheeling American privateers who raided Lunenburg and other shoreline communities, and the increased strength of the Halifax garrison after General William Howe withdrew British forces from Boston in 1776, combined to dampen the spirits of rebellion-minded Nova Scotians. While Halifax was bustling with military activity in anticipation of a possible Yankee attack, the local militias in outlining settlements such as Chester, Mahone Bay and Lunenburg were reinforced.

During and shortly after the years of the American War of Independence, Nova Scotia received another wave of new settlers. Many of these "Loyalists" were destitute, having lost everything, and were forced to manage as best they could, with some charitable help, in harsher environments of Halifax and surrounding areas. Others arrived in more fortunate circumstances and in time added a mixture of New England political and business savvy and even a touch of Southern charm to the life of the province. Among these was John Howe from Boston, who founded the *Journal* newspaper in Halifax in 1781 and whose son Joseph was to become a leading light in the political life of not only Nova Scotia but Canada as well.

With political and military issues resolved after the Treaty of Paris in 1783, the settlement around Chester prospered thanks to the industry of its early inhabitants, who made good use of the natural resources of the area. By 1784 it had become a thriving farming and

fishing community which could boast of several successful businesses, a strong militia, well-attended religious services and even a
Masonic lodge. Some of the arrivals from New England spread out
into the adjoining region to lots surveyed by the busy Charles
Morris. It was one of these settlers who would first discover the
treasure pit on Oak Island in 1795.

Meanwhile, the industrious German-speaking settlers, despite
hardships, Mi'kmaq raids and the slow-moving wheels of a distant
British administration, had established themselves around
Lunenburg. Along with a small French contingent, they gradually
turned the village into a busy settlement where the labours of farming and fishing families, skilled tradesmen and shrewd businessmen
brought steady progress and, in time, a good measure of prosperity.
Boatyards, storage sheds and repair shops sprung up along the busy
waterside. Eventually the town took on its own distinctive appearance with the construction of several large, decoratively designed
houses and imposing churches in the tradition of Rhineland architecture. St. John's Anglican, built under a royal charter in 1753, like St.
Paul's in Halifax had its framework supplied from Boston.

In the snug settlement of Mahone Bay, midway between
Lunenburg and Chester, a small group of New England settlers
arrived under the command of Ephriam Cook in 1754. With dogged
determination they cleared their tree-covered plots and worked hard
to gain some return from the sparse soil. Before long, they too
looked to the sea for sustenance and survival. The demands of fishing and maritime trade eventually resulted in the little town of
Mahone Bay building its own boatworks and other related businesses. The enterprising New Englanders who took up the land grants at
Western Shore, close to Oak Island, also divided their time and energy between the demands and rewards of surf and turf. Their activities soon expanded to include a lumber mill on the Vaughan River
and a cooperage by the water's edge, wooden ships and wooden bar-
rels then being the main means of transportation and storage. Prior
to the officially established settlements at Chester, Mahone Bay and
Lunenburg, several French families had been living in the LaHave
area near the site of a Mi'kmaq summer camp.

According to Judge Mather DesBrisay, author of *History of the
County of Lunenburg*, first published in 1870, Daniel McGinnis, the
New England settler who made the initial discovery of the Pit, took
up land on Oak Island. He was helped by young Anthony Vaughan,

whose father had come north from Rhode Island to work a two-hundred-acre holding in the area, and by John Smith who hailed from Boston and ended up farming on the island. Vaughan, aged about thirteen at the time of the discovery, later passed down a verbal account of the event to Robert Creelman and J.B. McCully, members of a group searching for the treasure in 1849; McGinnis and Smith also passed down their verbal accounts of the event. Creelman, in turn, lived until 1900, by which time several written accounts of the discovery had been recorded.

One of the earliest published accounts of the discovery is contained in a piece that was written by a member of the Oak Island Association in 1863 and printed in the *Colonist*, a Halifax newspaper, shortly afterwards. Another reliable account in print is contained in DesBrisay's *History*. DesBrisay grew up in Chester and had contact with those involved in the earliest attempts to find the treasure. In fact, the daughter of one of the men who first opened up the mysterious Pit on Oak Island lived with the DesBrisay family for some sixteen years. Although some variations are found in the various accounts, they are not major ones, and all agree on the essential details.

Early accounts differ as to whether or not the island was lived on at the time of the discovery of the treasure pit, but there is no doubt that several local settlers owned property on the island, which had been divided into thirty-two lots of four acres each. The original settlers would probably have utilized some of the excellent trees growing on the island, and its higher ground, once cleared, provided suitable areas for pasture and cultivation. The island was later farmed in at least three locations and a sawmill was built at its western end. With age, disease and cutting, all of the original oaks have long since disappeared.

3

The Treasure Hunt Begins

On an early summer day in 1795, Daniel McGinnis rowed across from the mainland and arrived on the southeast end of Oak Island. In his early twenties at the time, he may have been taking his first look at land he had recently acquired. He may also have been hunting wildlife or just taking a break from the daily round of back-breaking chores which were part and parcel of the lives of those settled in the area. Being young and of an obviously adventurous nature, he might also have been checking into the story told by the earlier settlers in Chester that strange lights had been repeatedly seen on the island at night and that two men from the village had rowed out to investigate but never returned. The highly superstitious and psychic nature of some of the early Nova Scotian settlers had probably added to the mystique surrounding the island. But this obviously did not deter McGinnis from investigating.

While walking through the stand of mature oak trees that covered much of the east end of the island, McGinnis was surprised to find a large, man-made clearing. Many of the trees had been cut down, leaving only the stumps, and new growth was beginning to take hold. His curiosity was aroused. Exploring further, he found a large circular indentation in the ground, about twelve feet in diameter, in the centre of the clearing. He also noticed that a large branch from one of the nearby trees protruded out over the hollow. One account of McGinnis's discovery of the Pit relates that this branch had a ship's pulley attached to it; another states there were strange markings cut into the base of the tree. A later account states that the clearing was covered with red clover and other plants not native to the island.

We can only imagine what thoughts raced through his mind at that moment. Likely they included the wild possibility that he had stumbled upon the hiding place of a pirate or privateer's treasure. He had good reason to think that such might be the case. The early colonists all along the eastern seaboard from Virginia to Nova Scotia had heard of the swashbuckling exploits of notorious buccaneers such as Sir Henry Morgan, Edward "Blackbeard" Teach and Captain William Kidd. All were supposed to have buried vast treasures in remote coves or on uninhabited islands. Many pirates had ports of call in Nova Scotia from 1650 to 1750. LaHave, just south of Mahone Bay and not very far from Oak Island, had been a safe haven for pirates at the turn of the century. They had readily joined with French naval forces to attack English shipping up and down the coast. Many documented accounts may be found of the exploits of pirates around Nova Scotia. If local legends are to be believed, the whole south shore of the province was a favourite resting and hiding place for pirates and their booty. In fact, the word *Mahone* may be derived from the French word *mahonne*, which comes from the Turkish word for a low-lying craft sometimes used by pirates in earlier days in the Mediterranean. It would have been logical for McGinnis to assume he had uncovered a pirate's cache.

Convinced he needed help in retrieving the treasure, McGinnis returned to the mainland and informed his two friends John Smith and Anthony Vaughan of his discovery. They went back to the island together, armed with shovels, and began to dig in the circularly shaped hollow area. After digging through the loose surface soil for about two feet, they hit a layer of flat stones. These stones, which they afterwards realized did not not come from the island, covered the entire opening. They were later believed to have been brought to the island from the Gold River area, about two miles away. After setting aside the stones, the enthusiastic diggers saw they were opening up a seven-foot-wide shaft that had been refilled. They dug through loose earth for another ten feet until they hit a solid floor of man-worked oak logs. The logs, six to eight inches in diameter, had been laid tightly together with their ends solidly embedded in the hard clay walls of the shaft. The logs were rotten on the outside, indicating they had been there for some time, and it was obvious to the young men that they had come from the trees cut down to create the clearing.

McGinnis and his friends also saw marks on the clay walls of the shaft left by implements used in the original digging operation. They eagerly prized free the logs and hauled them out of the pit, one by one, expecting to find a chest of some kind just below. What they found was a gap of two feet and more loose earth. After digging down ten more feet, they found themselves standing on yet another solid barrier of oak logs. By now exhausted but convinced they must be on the trail of a sizable treasure, they abandoned their attempt to excavate the shaft on their own and decided to seek help. Before leaving the site, they marked the depth reached and loosely refilled their excavation. Before leaving the island, they did some exploring and found a rough path running from the opposite side of the swamp to the western end of the island. At the nearby eastern cove, at low tide, they also found a large iron ringbolt embedded in a rock.

On returning to the mainland and telling the exciting story of their discovery, they found they could not interest others in joining them in the search. This is not so surprising when one considers that hardworking farmers and fishermen would have little time to devote to the questionable business of digging up buried treasure, especially on Oak Island. They were also strongly religious people who likely relied on the direction given them by the more educated and authoritative local clerics. Being somewhat superstitious, it is possible that the stories of strange lights and men disappearing would have been sufficient to frighten away some members of the community from setting foot on the island. Popular lore associating dead men's ghosts and ghoulish encounters with attempts to retrieve pirate treasure would also have thrown cold water on the idea of digging any further on Oak Island. Fear of military authorities might also have been a factor.

For whatever reason, McGinnis, Vaughan and Smith, in spite of their enthusiasm, could not interest others in their quest and may well have been warned not to proceed any further. However, on June 26th of that year, John Smith purchased Lot 18 on Oak Island from Casper Wollenhaupt, a Chester merchant, for the sum of five pounds. This lot encompassed the location of the treasure pit. He later purchased Lots 16 to 21 and built a house in the vicinity for himself and his family. According to all accounts, the Pit remained undisturbed and apparently a local secret for the next nine years.

It was 1803 before the first organized attempt was made to investigate the Oak Island Pit further. Simeon Lynds of Onslow decided to get involved after hearing about the mysterious discovery from his relative Anthony Vaughan during a visit to the area. Lynds belonged to a well-to-do family from the Truro area, at the head of the Bay of Fundy, many miles away from Oak Island. It is believed that he had had business in Chester and dropped in on his relations, the Vaughans. During the evening discussions the subject of the discovery on Oak Island had been brought up and the more sophisticated Lynds had expressed an interest in seeing the Pit. According to documented accounts, after spending some time on the island and viewing the site the following day, Lynds became convinced that a treasure had indeed been buried on Oak Island. On returning to his home in Onslow, Colchester County, his report of his observations persuaded his father and a few of his affluent and well-connected friends to invest in digging it up. These were not wild speculators, but men of fairly conservative dispositions; some were public figures and members of the Masonic Order. Lynds' comments must have been quite convincing. Among those who participated in the venture was Colonel Robert Archibald, a government surveyor who had laid out the township of Onslow in 1780 and later became town clerk and justice of the peace. Archibald was put in charge of operations on the island. His nephew Captain David Archibald, whose brother was later appointed speaker of the Assembly and attorney general for Nova Scotia, also joined the expedition. Another public figure involved was Sherrif Thomas Harris of Pictou County; the son of Dr. Thomas Harris, who had come to Pictou from Philadelphia in 1767, he too had been a surveyor before taking up the position of sheriff. So began the first of many commercial attempts to locate the treasure. As will be seen, it was also the beginning of a long involvement of prominent Freemasons in attempts to retrieve it.

Early in the summer of 1804, members of the treasure-hunting syndicate arrived on the island after sailing from near Onslow in a schooner loaded down with equipment and supplies. McGinnis, Smith and Vaughan joined them at the site and the dig began. During the intervening years the elements had caused the Pit to partially cave in, adding mud and debris to the fill on top of the platform at the twenty-foot level. In time they found the markers left by the three young local men years before. The second platform of logs was removed and the men cleared out another ten feet of loose earth. At the thirty-foot level the diggers came across another wooden barrier similar to those already encountered. They also discovered a layer of charcoal spread across the top of it. After removing these logs, which were also solidly embedded in the hard clay sides of the shaft, they dug down another ten feet until they were standing once again on a solid floor of oak logs. Here they found a covering of bluish putty-like clay, some of which was later used by the local men to glaze windows in their homes. A tier of smooth beach stones with strange figures and letters cut into them was discovered atop yet another log barrier at the fifty-foot level. We are told these made no sense to the diggers other than providing further indication that some vast treasure awaited them further down.

At the sixty-foot level the excavators were surprised to find a layer of manila grass and what looked like hemp or coconut fibre spread across another layer of logs. According to one eyewitness account, bushels of the fibrous material were hauled out of the Pit. Knowing that coconut fibre had been used as dunnage for the safe storage of cargo in ships up to that time, and that it would likely have originated in the Caribbean, some of the excited treasure hunters instantly concluded that this indicated one of two possibilities: a cache of pirate's treasure or Spanish gold from warmer territories to the south.

The pace of the digging picked up until another unexpected discovery was made, this time at the ninety-foot level. A large, unusual-looking flat stone slab was found in the centre of the wooden floor. It was about two-and-a-half feet in length, one-and-a-quarter feet wide and ten inches thick, and its olive tint gave it an appearance unlike any other stone they had ever seen before. It was later confirmed to be not indigenous to the island and to be a slab of yellow-tinged Swedish granite. After hauling this unexpected find to the surface and turning it over, the men saw strange markings carved on one side. The two lines of cryptic writing, made up of shapes which included crosses, triangles, dots, squares and circles, were apparently indecipherable to those present, even though similar to traditional Masonic symbols. This unusual stone and its enigmatic message were enthusiastically accepted as convincing evidence of a substantial treasure buried further below. Some thought the treasure must surely lie just below the wooden barrier where the inscribed stone had been found.

The digging began again, the local men more enthused than ever at the prospect of becoming rich. With night approaching, they quickly removed the ninety-foot barrier only to find more loose earth beneath. This time, however, the earth was becoming moist and water was beginning to appear. They worked their way through it for several feet without finding anything. Before finishing for the day, they carried out their usual procedure of probing down into the earth below with an iron bar. At ninety-eight feet they struck a solid object and heard a sound they had not come across in their previous probes. Some of the men were convinced they had tapped on a large wooden chest. Weary but encouraged, the men left for the night, sure that in the morning they would finish the job and uncover the treasure.

Early the next day they returned to the site only to find the Pit filled with water to within thirty feet of the surface. Sixty feet of muddy water separated them from the treasure they had almost placed their hands upon the night before. Archibald immediately ordered the water baled out, and the men set to work, laboriously hauling bucket after bucket to the surface. In spite of their untiring efforts, they could not reduce the water level to any noticeable degree and it was eventually realized that another approach was needed to solve the problem. All work came to a halt and the project was put on hold until the fall.

Disappointed but not despairing, Lynds and Colonel Archibald consulted a Mr. Mosher, an engineering type from Newport, Hants County. Mosher recommended that a large bailing pump be constructed and put to work on the site. By September the group was back on the island, and the pump, which cost the princely sum of eighty English pounds, was lowered into the Pit until it rested on the floor at the ninety-foot level. The new pump broke down before any water even trickled out of the hose at the surface and the frustrated Lynds and the other investors decided to postpone any further work until the following year.

Still convinced a worthwhile treasure awaited them, the dedicated Onslow investors returned to Oak Island in the spring of 1805. On Archibald's advice, it was agreed to sink a new shaft some fifteen feet to the east of the original one. By having a crew of local men dig down to about 110 feet and then tunnel laterally under the Pit, it was hoped they could reach the treasure from beneath and bring it safely to surface. This was an arduous and time-consuming task, given that they were digging through hard clay. Eventually they reached the 110-foot level, encountering neither obstacles nor water. They began to tunnel in the direction of the treasure pit and were within two feet of reaching it when the dry soil ahead of them began to turn to mud, and water burst through with unrelenting force. The men scrambled to make their way back through the narrow tunnel and up and out of the new shaft as the water flooded in behind them. All managed to get out safely, but looking back down into the shaft they saw the water was rising rapidly. They helplessly watched as it finally settled not far from the surface, matching the level in the original Pit.

By now a good deal of time and money had been expended in the search. The disappointed members of the Onslow Company had little to show for their efforts. With their collective investment gone, the principals chose to abandon the project. However, their efforts had provided indisputable evidence that someone had given a lot of thought and gone to a lot of trouble to hide what could only be a significant treasure on Oak Island. Unfortunately, nature, in the form of an underground watercourse, had come between them and the cache, or so it seemed. The Onslow Company went out of existence and the three discoverers of the pit, McGinnis, Smith and Vaughan, got on with their day-to-day lives. Having purchased some additional land, Smith built himself a farmhouse on the island and used the hieroglyphically inscribed stone slab as a solid backing for his fireplace. To this day, the cove below the site of the farm is known as Smith's Cove (although that may be because an earlier title holder also had the same name). Vaughan returned to help out on his family's large holding on the mainland at nearby Western Shore, where successive generations have lived up to the present time. McGinnis held onto his land grant on the island and a family home was later built there. Such were the circumstances and the events surrounding the initial discovery of the Pit and the first coordinated attempt to retrieve the treasure.

This attempt, although unsuccessful, had produced some dramatic circumstantial evidence that a treasure of some kind was present on the island. It had also raised new questions about the treasure's possible origin and nature. It was now obvious that an organized and somewhat skilled work force had been involved in burying it and there was more to this treasure than first thought. Members of the Onslow syndicate must have suspected as much: at least one of them would reinvest in the next attempt to find it, more than forty years later.

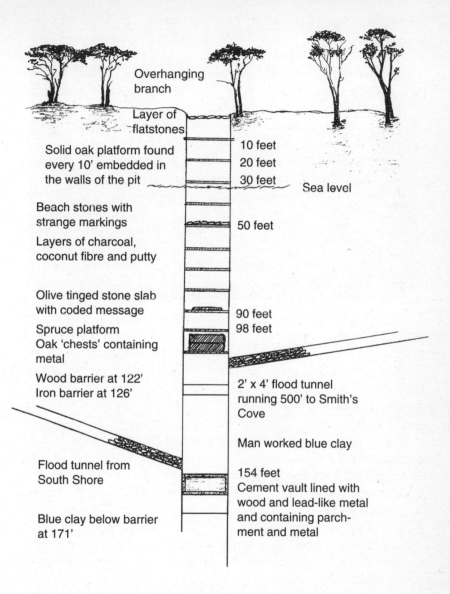

Overhanging branch

Layer of flatstones

Solid oak platform found every 10' embedded in the walls of the pit

Beach stones with strange markings

Layers of charcoal, coconut fibre and putty

Olive tinged stone slab with coded message

Spruce platform
Oak 'chests' containing metal

Wood barrier at 122'
Iron barrier at 126'

Flood tunnel from South Shore

Blue clay below barrier at 171'

10 feet
20 feet
30 feet

Sea level

50 feet

90 feet
98 feet

2' x 4' flood tunnel running 500' to Smith's Cove

Man worked blue clay

154 feet
Cement vault lined with wood and lead-like metal and containing parchment and metal

Discoveries made in the Treasure Pit from 1795 to 1900. The Pit was found in a clearing on the east end of the island.

Inscribed stone found at 90 foot level in the Treasure Pit in 1803.

4

Treasure Chests and Water Traps

The Truro Company was formed in 1845 by a group of area businessmen who were convinced they could retrieve the treasure. In the years since the attempts made by the Onslow Company, advances had been made in excavating and pumping technologies, and the principals of the new syndicate were certain they had both the equipment and expertise necessary to capitalize on their investment. Anthony Vaughan and John Smith were still alive, as was Sheriff Thomas Harris of Pictou who again invested in the enterprise. A Dr. Lynds of Truro, likely a relation of Simeon Lynds, was also involved, as were John Gammell and Robert Creelman of Upper Stewiacke. The Masonic involvement continued through Creelman, Lynds and Harris. Creelman had obtained first-hand accounts of the initial discovery and the earlier dig from Smith and Vaughan (and this information was also used to assist later operations in 1863 and 1893 as Creelman continued his interest). Jotham McCully of Truro was made manager of the present operation, and James Pitblado, an experienced mining engineer, was appointed foreman.

For financial or perhaps other reasons, the actual work did not commence on the island until the summer of 1849. Arrangements were entered into with John Smith, who owned the land encompassing the treasure pit. Aided by Anthony Vaughan, now age sixty-seven, the enthusiastic treasure hunters located the Pit and commenced clean-up operations. Both the Pit and the adjacent shaft excavated under Archibald's direction in 1805 had been filled in for safety. The elements had also been at work: both holes had caved in and become filled with debris. Excavation began in the original Pit under Pitblado's supervision. After getting down about six feet, the men found part of the pump that had failed the earlier searchers. After twelve days of persistent labour they succeeded in reaching the eighty-six-foot level, where some of the earlier cribbing remained intact. The water that had previously been such a problem seemed to have disappeared. An eyewitness account written down by a member of the syndicate and later published in the *Colonist* in Halifax on January 7, 1864, describes what happened next:

> They found that it remained exactly as discovered by Lynds (in 1804) and did not entertain the shadow of a doubt in their own minds, but that the Pit had been sunk by some parties long before Lynds ever saw the place. They worked on successfully for about a fortnight when Saturday night arrived and all further work was postponed until Monday morning. Sabbath morning came and no sign of water, more than usual, appearing in the pit, when men left for church at Chester with lighter hearts. At two o'clock they returned from church, and to their great surprise found water standing in the pit to the depth of sixty feet, being on a level with that in the bay. The next morning they set vigorously to work bailing, and had not been long engaged until the result appeared as unsatisfactory as taking soup with a fork. Notwithstanding the disappointment was great and the problem seemed insurmountable, they did not feel disposed to drop the work without further efforts.

Water was once again sitting in the Pit thirty feet from the surface, and no amount of bailing made any difference. Undeterred, McCully ordered a platform installed just above the water and attempts were made to explore the depths by means of a pod auger, a primitive drill used in mining operations. Under McCully's supervision, five separate holes were drilled by the auger to a depth of about 106 feet from the surface. The first hole was sunk just west of the centre of the shaft and the others east of it. The first two drillings produced no tangible results, but the treasure hunters soon had reason to become excited. McCully took notes and some years later described the proceedings in a written statement:

> The platform [found in the Pit in 1804] was struck at 98 feet just as the old diggers found it when sounding with the iron bar. After going through the platform, which was five inches thick, and proved to be of spruce, the auger dropped twelve inches and then went through twelve inch-

es of oak; then it went through twenty two inches of metal in pieces; but the auger failed to bring up anything in the nature of treasure, except three links resembling the links of an ancient watch chain. It then went through eight inches of oak, which was thought to be the bottom of the first box and the top of the next; then twenty two inches of metal, the same as before; then four inches of oak and six inches of spruce, then into clay seven feet without striking anything.

In boring a second hole, the platform was struck, as before, at 98 feet; passing through this, the auger fell about eighteen inches and came in contact with [as supposed] the side of a chest. The flat chisel revolving close to the side of the cask gave it a jerky and irregular motion. On withdrawing the auger, several splinters of oak [believed to be from a bilge of a cask] such as might come from the side of an oak stave, a piece of hoop made of birch and a small quantity of a brown fibrous substance, closely resembling the husk of a coconut, were brought up. The difference between the upper and lower platforms was found to be six feet.

The small piece of linked chain was described by McCully as being made of gold and similar to the chain from a uniform's epaulet. These discoveries heightened the conviction of the shareholders that treasure definitely awaited them in the watery depths of the Pit. Their conclusion was that two oaken chests filled with precious metal rested, one on top of the other, on a six-inch-thick spruce platform at a depth of about 105 feet.

The furtive actions of their foreman Pitblado on the same day and his subsequent behaviour no doubt fuelled their imaginations even further. Pitblado had been instructed to carefully remove every bit of material brought to the surface by the auger and to preserve everything so all material could be later examined under a microscope. On the basis of what had just been discovered, Pitblado was ordered to make a fifth and final boring. Gammell, one of the larger shareholders in the company, later claimed that he saw the foreman take something from the auger when he thought no one was watching, wash it and, after examining it closely, put it into his pocket. On being questioned by Gammell at the time, Pitblado refused to show him what

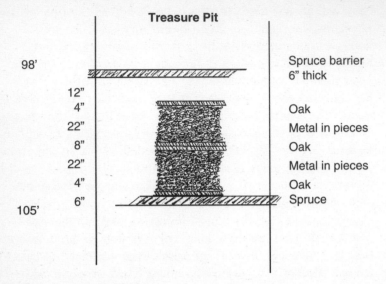

Treasure Pit

98'

12"
4"
22"
8"
22"
4"
6"

105'

Spruce barrier
6" thick

Oak
Metal in pieces
Oak
Metal in pieces
Oak
Spruce

Drilled through in 1849.

he had found but promised to produce it for all to see at the next directors' meeting. The wily foreman failed to show up at that meeting. Instead he quit his position at Oak Island and approached Charles Archibald, manager of the Acadian Iron Works in Londonderry, Nova Scotia, with a proposition to recover the treasure. The information provided by the renegade foreman led Archibald to make a determined but unsuccessful attempt to purchase the eastern end of the island. Archibald later moved to England and Pitblado disappeared into oblivion, having pocketed what was believed to have been a small but significant clue concerning the treasure.

Although little evidence concerning the actual nature of the treasure was found, there was now substantial and incontrovertible proof that a deep underground operation undoubtedly involving many men and much labour had been undertaken in the past on Oak Island for the purpose of concealing boxes or chests, the origins and contents of which remained unknown. Now more than ever before was there solid reason to believe that this action had been carried out to hide something of extraordinary value. Summer turned to fall, and with the days growing shorter and the weather less obliging, all work at the site was suspended for the year. Throughout the winter months the men from Truro reviewed their discoveries, discussed their conclusions and made plans for another assault on the treasure the following year.

Work recommenced on the site in the spring of 1850 with the sinking of another shaft, the third in the area, about ten feet west of the treasure pit. The plan was to dig to a level below the area where the chests rested, tunnel laterally into the original Pit and allow the water to drain into the new and deeper shaft, thereby making the treasure more accessible. Aware of the near tragedy experienced in a similar escapade in 1805, the men proceeded cautiously. However, when they were finally within a few feet of finishing the operation, water burst through the clay, forcing the workmen to retreat rapidly through the tunnel and scramble out of the pit to safety on the surface. Before long there was forty-five feet of water in the new shaft. The continuous operation of two two-horse gin balers in both the shafts over a period of a week failed to reduce the water level in the treasure pit below the eighty-foot mark. Nature seemed determined to undermine their every effort. It was time for the excavators to stand back and think anew about the problem they faced.

It was during this time that someone discovered the water in the Pit was not only salty but also rose and fell with the tide. Some thought was given to the fact that water had only shown up in the treasure pit after the earlier treasure seekers had reached below the ninety-foot platform, the level where the inscribed stone slab had been found. No water had appeared in either of the additional shafts, even though they were dug through the same type of soil, in the same area and to the same depth as the original Pit. It was only after attempts had been made to tunnel laterally to the location of the treasure that water had burst through. So, if the water was entering by natural means, how was the treasure pit dug in the first place?

The men from Truro deducted that the water flooding the treasure pit must be entering through a man-made tunnel from somewhere near the shore. Discussions also arose about whether the inscribed stone had contained a coded warning and instructions on how to avoid the flooding. The crew was put to work investigating the shore at Smith's Cove about five hundred feet east of the treasure pit for signs of an inflow source somewhere in the rocks. This led to a startling discovery which left the treasure hunters scratching their heads in amazement at the ingenuity of the originator of the underground workings on the island and the extent of his or her determination to keep unwanted intruders away from the treasure.

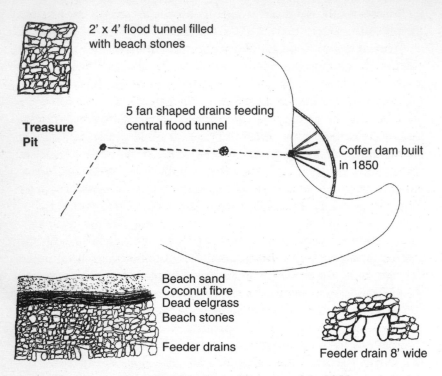

2' x 4' flood tunnel filled
with beach stones

5 fan shaped drains feeding
central flood tunnel

**Treasure
Pit**

Coffer dam built
in 1850

Beach sand
Coconut fibre
Dead eelgrass
Beach stones

Feeder drains

Feeder drain 8' wide

Flooding system from Smith's Cove. Discovered in 1850.

On examining the beach area, the men noticed for the first time that most of the larger stones had been removed from the centre area and that, as the tide ebbed, rivulets of water oozed from several places in the beach close to the low water mark. One recorded description was that the beach "gulched forth water like a sponge being squeezed." The crew was ordered to investigate and, after digging down some three feet into the sand, they came across a layer of brown, fibrous material, the same as had been found in the Pit. This layer of coconut fibre was almost two inches thick. Below it the men found a four-inch-thick layer of decayed eelgrass or kelp. Tons of this material were removed and piled in stacks like haycocks along the shore. These labours uncovered a compact bed of beach stones below, extending for about 145 feet along the shore, from the low to high water marks. It was obvious to the excavators that this was not a normal condition, and in order to investigate the matter further, they build a coffer dam, a semicircular seawall, to hold back the tide.

Working in the dried-out area, they discovered that the clay bed of the beach had been removed and beach stones had been deposited in the excavated area. On removing some of these stones, the men were astonished to find five perfectly formed box drains, each one approximately eight inches in width, made of flat stones laid along the sides and across the top, embedded in the beach. Further exploration revealed that the five drains extended out along the entire 145-foot area in a finger-like fan formation. Running back from the edge of the ocean and dropping deeper as they approached the shoreline, the drains converged on each other over a much larger, funnel-like central drain just above the high water mark. An article in the *Colonist* some years later gave the following account of this discovery:

> In investigating the drains they found that they connected to one of larger dimensions, the stones forming which had been prepared with a hammer, and were mechanically laid in such a way that the drain could not collapse. There were a number of tiers of stones strengthening the higher part of the drain, on the top of which was also found a coating of the same sort of grass as that already noticed. Over it came a layer of blue sand, such as before had not been seen on the island, and over the sand was spread the gravel indigenous to the coast. Having laid bare the large drain for a short distance into the bank, they found it had been so well made and protected that no earth had sifted through the arch to obstruct water passing through it. Then they attempted to follow the inward direction of the drain, in search of a perpendicular shaft, but on account of the surrounding soil being so soft, and so much saturated with water, it was given up as impracticable.

Other eyewitness accounts later recorded also confirm this discovery. It was obvious to the members of the Truro Company that they had uncovered the source of the flooding in the treasure pit. What was mind-boggling was the extensiveness and ingenuity of the treasure-burying operation. Someone had gone to the trouble to construct a coffer dam to hold back the tides; remove the stones, sand and clay from the original beach; inlay the drains and encase them in a solid bed of beach stones; cover this with layers of eelgrass and coconut fibre; and then replace the sand, leaving the impression of a normal beach. The members of the Truro Company marvelled, as many others have since, at the cleverly simple but highly effective nature of the operation. Seawater was running inland under the beach by means of tidal pressure and gravity along a well-engineered system of drains, then dropping further underground as it flowed in from the shore at Smith's Cove to a point more than five hundred feet inland, where it connected with the treasure pit somewhere below the ninety-five-foot level. The installation process had obviously involved much planning and labour. Even more remarkable were the mathematically precise engineering calculations needed to make the system operate effectively.

Deductions from the evidence uncovered made it clear that the flooding system had only been built or made operative after the treasure had been deposited below the ninety-foot level in the Pit. A series of pressure-resistant seals made of oak logs and other materials had been systematically installed from the bottom up. These seals also prevented the infill from collapsing downwards. The Pit was then capped with a cover of flat stones and surface soil. Then and only then was the coffer dam removed and the seawater allowed to run its course until it was held back somewhere along the flood tunnel by the air pressure created by the seals in the treasure pit. The designer of this flood trap obviously had to know in advance that his air versus water pressure calculations were accurate. Otherwise he would have flooded his own treasure and the whole operation would have ended in disaster right at the start.

Although the unexpected discovery of such a well-engineered and executed flooding system caused those involved in 1850 to marvel, it also led them to conclude that they now had a better chance of reaching the treasure because they could now cut the water off at its source and prevent any more flooding of the Pit. Unfortunately, as had happened before and was to happen again, nature intervened in the form of a fierce storm and an unusually high tide. The costly coffer dam collapsed and the exposed man-made workings on the beach were recovered with sand.

A decision was made to try to locate the large single flood tunnel running underground from the shoreline to the Pit, rather than incur the expense of rebuilding the coffer dam. They were sure they could then block off the flow of water entering the Pit. A point was selected about 140 feet east of the treasure pit on a line between it and the intake location on the shore. A shaft was sunk seventy-five feet without success. Then a second attempt was made twelve feet to the south. At a depth of thirty-five feet they encountered a large boulder and, on trying to pry it loose, salt water gushed in and filled the shaft to tide level. Elated by their apparent success, the men quickly sank heavy timbers down into the bottom of the shaft to prevent any more water from flowing through.

However, when they recommenced pumping operations in the Pit, they were horrified to find that their efforts had been ineffective. A mass of water still stood between them and the treasure. Undeterred, they proceeded to dig another shaft about eighteen feet south of the treasure pit, to a depth of 118 feet, deeper that any previous shaft, in another attempt to drain the original Pit. After reaching the required depth, they drove a three-by-four-foot tunnel towards a point directly under the position of the treasure. Before reaching their destination, the men took a well-earned dinner break, during which disaster struck. A loud crashing noise brought the men running to the open face of the treasure pit. When the dust and debris had settled, they were horrified to find that the bottom had dropped out of the Pit, causing the wooden cribbing on the shaft walls to collapse. The two chests or boxes containing the hoped-for treasure had fallen further down into the Pit and now lay buried under a mountain of broken lumber. Mud and debris had also flooded into the new shaft, filling it to a depth of twelve feet. One workman, who had had the misfortune to be in the tunnel at the time of the collapse had managed to salvage a dish-shaped piece of yellow-painted wood which had landed at his feet as he ran for safety. This led to speculation that the treasure chests or boxes may have been swept into the connecting tunnel and ended up elsewhere underground.

The disaster proved to be the final straw for the Truro Company. Its capital was now gone and, in spite of the exciting discovery of the flooding system, appeals for additional funds met with a poor response. The company finally folded in 1854, the task of recovering the treasure having proved to be too difficult and expensive.

Nonetheless, the discovery of the elaborate man-made workings under the beach and the water traps suggested the presence of a truly fantastic treasure on Oak Island that continued to lure men to its shores. The search for the elusive treasure, however, would eventually cost more than money. It would cost several lives.

5

The Mystery Deepens

In 1857, Henry Poole, a Nova Scotia geologist, visited Oak Island. His observations are contained in a report submitted to the government of the day:

> I crossed to Oak Island and observed slate all the way along the main shore, but I could not see any rock in situ on the island. I went to the spot where people had been engaged for so many years searching for the supposed treasure of Captain Kidd. I found the original shaft had caved in, and two others had been sunk alongside. One was open and said to be 120 feet deep, and in all that depth no rock had been struck. The excavated matter alongside was composed of sand and boulder rocks and though the pit was some two hundred yards from the shore, the water in the shaft (which I measured to be within thirty three feet of the top) rose and fell with the tide, showing a free communication between the sea and the shaft.

In 1859, while hordes of gold hungry prospectors were digging and panning for instant fortunes on the banks of the Fraser River and in the Cariboo region of British Columbia, there was renewed interest in the fortune still waiting to be found on Oak Island. A.L. Spedon, who visited the island in 1862 and wrote about it in his *Rambles Among the Bluenoses*, indicates that additional activity went on at the site after the official departure of the Truro Company in 1850. This likely involved members of this same Truro syndicate.

According to Spedon, during the summer of 1859 no less than thirty horses were engaged in working pumps in an effort to reduce the water level in the Pit, but all efforts proved hopeless. In the fall of 1861, at great expense, pumps were erected to be driven by steam power, but scarcely had the work commenced when the boiler burst, causing operations to be suspended until another season.

This accident had also caused the first fatality on the island connected to the treasure search. When that boiler had burst, one man had been scalded to death and several others had been injured. In spite of the tragedy and the company's failure to lower the water in the Pit, Spedon had seen enough to conclude that there really was a treasure buried on Oak Island.

In the meantime, the whole island had come into the possession of Anthony Graves. In 1853 John Smith had deeded his property on the east end to his two sons. Either because they lacked their father's conviction regarding buried treasure or for other reasons, they sold the land four years later to Henry Stevens. He in turn sold it to Anthony Graves, who by 1863 had built himself a house and barns on the north side of the island near Joudrey's Cove, well away from the site of the treasure pit.

Several of the individuals who had invested in the 1848-50 Truro Company had obviously not lost their enthusiasm and conviction in relation to Oak Island. By 1863 they were ready and able to recommit financially to the project, and so the Oak Island Association was formed. Again there was Masonic interest involved. Among the investors were Robert Creelman, Adams A. Tupper, J.B. McCully and James McNutt, who kept a written record of the work. They entered into an agreement with Anthony Graves, whereby he would receive one-third the value of any treasure found.

Sixty-three men, thirty-three horses and four seventy-gallon bailing casks were used in an all-out attempt to clean out and pump dry the treasure pit and two other shafts nearby. The plan was again to get at the treasure from below.

After two days of continuous work they had succeeded in reducing the water to the eighty-two-foot level. Then one of the connecting tunnels filled up with mud and the water rose in the Pit again. The plan ended in dismal and costly failure when it was noticed that the Pit bottom had sunk several feet and the wooden cribbing had shifted dangerously. It was then decided to sink two more shafts west of the original one in attempts to intercept the water tunnel, but these also ended in failure. The company's resources were then put to use to block off the inflow of seawater from under the beach at Smith's Cove. Much of the sand was cleared off and the stone drains were filled with clay. This proved to be partially successful until the incoming tide washed away the clay. With their finances and optimism rapidly decreasing, the directors made a bold decision. They ordered yet another shaft, the ninth, to be dug a hundred feet southeast of the treasure pit, to a depth of 120 feet. Tunnels were then driven in various directions. One of them entered the original Pit at the one-hundred-foot level, just below where the treasure chests had rested. Further investigations of the Pit revealed the presence of a partially solid floor at the 108-foot level. They also seemed to confirm earlier speculation that the treasure, along with the platform or trap it had rested on, had slid through the adjoining tunnel into the second shaft dug to a depth of 110 feet in 1805. The wooden chests, however, could still not be located.

Still confident of impending success but in urgent need of a fresh infusion of cash, the company held a public meeting, which was reported in a Halifax newspaper in 1863:

> A meeting of The Oak Island Association was held at Dalhousie College. The secretary of the Association, Mr. J. B. McCully, stated that they calculated to reach the treasure in fourteen days. The expenses of carrying on the work were $50 per day. The company was considerably in debt, but the directors were endeavouring to sell enough shares to raise $500. Thirty shares of $5 each were subscribed for at that meeting.

Apart from renewing public interest in the mystery, the meeting had failed to have its desired effect and the company could only carry out sporadic and inconclusive work during the following year. The Oak Island Association finally ceased operations in 1865.

However, within a year the Oak Island Eldorado Company, also known as the Halifax Company, was formed. New investors and some of the previous ones together raised $4,000. James McNutt was again on hand to record the progress or lack of it. The company's prospectus outlined its plan of action, which was to build a substantial seawall in Smith's Cove to hold out the water and block the inlet from the sea. The prospectus went on to claim "there cannot be any doubt but that this mode of operation must succeed and will lead to the development of the treasure so long sought for." The gargantuan task of enclosing the cove with a 12-foot-high, 375-foot-long coffer dam, the second such attempt, ended in failure and with the loss of half of the company's capital when the wood and clay structure was swept away by the tides. It seemed the elements were against anyone finding the treasure.

Failing to stem the inflow of water from the beach, the company then focused its attention on the treasure pit itself and pumped it dry down to the 108-foot level. Here one of the workmen, while tunnelling in the direction of the oaken chests, encountered a water-filled cavity beneath the tunnel. The pressure of the water rising up into the Pit made further investigation impossible. The company then decided to do some exploratory drilling from a platform installed at the ninety-foot level, but the results were inconclusive. They then made another attempt to divert the water flooding in from the sea by sinking a shaft about one hundred feet southeast of the treasure pit. From about 110 feet down in this, the tenth shaft dug on the island, they drove a series of lateral tunnels in the direction of the supposed flood tunnel and the treasure pit itself. In correspondence dated June 1895, the company's manager S.C. Fraser described their discovery:

The Halifax Company's work was at a base of 110 feet, except two circling tunnels which were on a higher level. As we entered the old place of the treasure (by a tunnel) we cut off the mouth of the `pirate tunnel'. As we opened it, the water hurled around rocks about twice the size of a man's head, with many smaller, and drove the men back for protection. We could not go into the shaft again for about nine hours. Then the pumps conquered and we went down and cleared it out. The (pirate) tunnel was found near the top of our tunnel. I brought Mr. Hill, the engineer, down and he put his arm into the hole of the tunnel, up to his shoulder. It was made of round stones, such as are found abundantly on the beach and fields around the island. Where we found it was the mouth of it, where it empties onto the treasure, before it, the treasure, went down [during the collapse in the Pit in 1850].

To confirm that they had in fact found the exit of the flood tunnel, cartloads of clay were dumped on the beach in the vicinity of the tunnel's entrance and, sure enough, the water in the Pit was muddied. This discovery established beyond doubt that a man-made tunnel, measuring little more than two by four feet and with a grade of about twenty-two degrees, extended downwards from the beach area over a distance of 500 feet to enter the treasure pit at a depth of 110 feet. Attempts to locate a gate in this channel proved unsuccessful. There was by now evidence that an open space or chamber was present below this level in the Pit area. The members of the Halifax Company concluded that the treasure had probably collapsed into this water-filled cavern and was now well out of their reach.

By 1867 the company's finances were exhausted. After securing a platform at the thirty-foot level and filling in the treasure pit, the workmen were let go, and Creelman, McCully and the others reluctantly left the island. However, some of them were to return more than twenty-five years later for another try, joined by a man who was to devote almost sixty years of his life to trying to get to the bottom of the Oak Island mystery. He would also maintain the Masonic interest in the island's enigmatic treasure.

6

A Vault and Parchment

There seems to have been little or no treasure-hunting activity on the island between 1867 and 1893. During this time an ox being used for ploughing by Anthony Grave's daughter Sophia Sellers fell into a large hole which opened up midway between the treasure pit and Smith's Cove. This hole was later discovered to be a man-made air shaft connected to the flood tunnel that ran in from the beach. Other discoveries included an old ship's whistle made of ivory found near the shoreline and a heavy copper coin with strange markings dated 1713. During this time, Anthony Graves is said to have often paid for merchandise in Mahone Bay using Spanish money. Some years after his death, a Spanish silver coin dated 1785 and several diggings were found on his property, indicating that Graves had been involved in a treasure hunt of his own and been successful.

In 1893, Frederick Blair of Amherst, Nova Scotia, helped to rekindle interest and attract new investors in the Oak Island project. He had been introduced to the mystery by his uncle Isaac Blair, and Jefferson McDonald, both of whom had worked on the island in earlier years. A meticulous researcher, Blair made it his business to acquire as much verbal and written information as he could from people previously associated with the treasure search. Assisted by the experienced engineer Adams Tupper, who had himself met with Anthony Vaughan, one of the discovers of the Pit, he drew up an appealing prospectus. It gave a detailed history of the previous attempts to retrieve the treasure and optimistically offered a straightforward solution to the water problem:

> It is perfectly obvious that the great mistake thus far has been in attempting to bail out the ocean through the various pits. The present company intends to use the best modern appliances for cutting off the flow of water through the tunnel at some point near the shore, before attempting to pump out the water. It believes, from investigations already made, that such an attempt will be com-

pletely successful, and if it is there can be no trouble in
pumping out the Money Pit as dry as when the treasure
was first placed there.

Several earlier investors joined the new company, an indication
of their conviction that treasure existed somewhere down in the Pit
and that Blair's approach using more modern equipment would succeed. With an insurance office in Boston and a flair for salesman-
ship, Blair then succeeded in attracting several New Englanders to
the project. One of them, A.M. Bridgman of Brockton,
Massachusetts, became president of the new company. Among the
Nova Scotia shareholders were William Chappell, who ran a lumber
business in Amherst, Captain Richard Lowerison and Captain John
W. Welling. Chappell, like several of the others involved, was
knowledgeable of Masonic symbolism and would have shared in
any secret perception about the Oak Island mystery unknown to
those outside the fraternity. Adams Tupper was put in charge of
operations on the ground. Between them they raised $60,000, half of
which was used to take out a three-year lease on the property from
the Sellers family. Labourers were hired locally, necessary buildings
were constructed and work commenced in the summer of 1894.
Blair kept meticulous notes of the activities of the company over the
next four years.

The men first spent some time exploring the large hole, east of
the treasure pit, into which the Seller's ox had fallen some years
before. Afterwards called the "Cave-in Pit," it had been filled in
with boulders. When these were removed, it was found to be a six-
foot-wide circular shaft which dropped to a depth of fifty-two feet.
The next day, seawater burst through from the flood tunnel and rose
to tide level. The conclusion was that this had been an air shaft used
in the construction of the flood tunnel. It was considered too unsafe
to work in and so was abandoned. An unsuccessful attempt was then
made to cut off the flow of seawater to the treasure pit by blowing
up the flood tunnel with dynamite. Various earlier shafts were
explored in the hope of finding an underground passageway into the
original Pit. This approach also ended in failure and nearly cost two
of the workmen their lives. In September 1895 the company was
forced to raise additional funds to purchase a new steam pump and
boiler. Captain Welling was put in charge of the operations, and during the next eighteen months various attempts were made to either

block off the water or enter the original Pit from below.

In March 1897 the second death connected to the treasure search occurred. A workman named Maynard Kaiser attempted to ride to the surface of one of the pits on a bailing cask. The extra weight caused the rope to slip from the overhead pulley and he fell to his death. Many of the local workmen left the island and refused to come back. In a Halifax newspaper report of the inquest, it was pointed out that the coroner's jury exonerated the management from all blame and added this unusual note: "Captain Welling, who is in charge of the work of excavating for the Oak Island treasure reports that all his men have quit the job. They became suspicious after the death of poor Kaiser last week and will not continue to dig. One of the men had a dream in which the spirit of Captain Kidd appeared and warned him they would all be dead if they continued the search."

Operations on the site came to a standstill and Welling was forced to hire new labourers in Halifax. Soon afterwards they succeeded in relocating the original treasure pit, which had been covered up by the Halifax Company. When it was pumped dry enough for the workmen to descend to the 110-foot level, they also found the stone-filled flood tunnel. Their observations confirmed that it had indeed been cut through hard clay and was very well constructed. More pump trouble resulted in the Pit being refilled with seawater and work had to be curtailed.

Frustrated in their attempt to locate the treasure in the depths of the original Pit, and with money in short supply, the Halifax Company then decided on a last desperate plan to block off the flow of seawater from the beach. Five narrow holes were drilled along the shoreline. Each hole was more than eighty feet deep and about fifty feet up from the high water mark. Dynamite was then dropped into the holes and detonated. Over 150 pounds of explosives was used in the centre hole, the one directly over the supposed line of the flood tunnel. After the blast the water at the thirty-foot level in the treasure pit and in the "Cave-in Pit" boiled up for some time and then settled. The men were convinced that they had at last blocked off the flood tunnel, and work recommenced in the treasure pit.

The water in the Pit was pumped out to the one-hundred-foot level and a platform was installed from which to continue searching for the treasure, believed to be in the general locality. A team of drillers set up equipment on this platform and began to probe the depths below. Their drillings produced some very startling and unexpected results that were witnessed by several of the officials present. Wood was drilled through several times below 120 feet, leading to the conclusion.that in 1850 the Pit had collapsed further than originally thought. Iron was also struck on the way down. Then the most dramatic discovery of all: at 153 feet the drill went through seven inches of what seemed to be cement, then through five inches of oak. The auger then dropped a couple of inches and came to rest embedded in what the drillers believed to be loose metal in pieces.

When the auger was carefully withdrawn and the borings minutely examined by Putman, Chappell, Welling and others, a most unexpected discovery was made. A small piece of ancient parchment was found among oak chips and coconut husks. The treasure searchers were naturally surprised by these discoveries. For some it may have been the confirmation they had been waiting for, that there was more to the Oak Island treasure than pirate booty.

Additional drillings established, at least in the minds of those present, that at 153 feet a cement-like vault at least seven feet high and with walls seven inches thick lay below. Inside was a smaller container, the oak walls of which were five inches thick. It held loose metal of some kind and a manuscript, or documents, as evidenced by the piece of parchment brought to the surface. All attempts at procuring a sample of the loose metal failed. Drilling beyond this cement vault, the men came across eleven feet of blue puddled clay, similar to that discovered years before higher up in the Pit. At 171 feet the drill again struck iron, this time so hard that three hours of drilling could not penetrate it. Filings were pumped up to the surface and tested with a magnet. Another drilling at a slight angle bypassed the iron obstruction and reached a depth of 188 feet. All these discoveries astonished Blair, Chappell and their partners. No one had expected to find another treasure load, and certainly not one as mysterious as this. Naturally they were quite excited and encouraged by the discovery. However, one of the exploratory drillings had also given them cause for concern. In one hole the drill had entered a channel at 126 feet from which water had gushed to the surface at a rate of four hundred gallons per minute, indicating yet another flood tunnel.

Two samples of the cement-like material were sent to A. Boake Roberts and Company of London, England, a company that specialized in chemical analysis, with the request to confirm whether it was

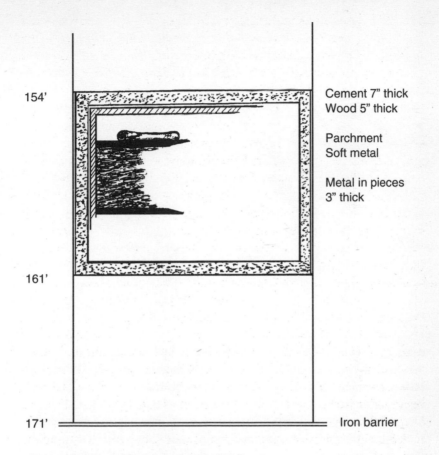

154'

Cement 7" thick
Wood 5" thick

Parchment
Soft metal

Metal in pieces
3" thick

161'

171'   Iron barrier

Cement vault drilled through in 1897.

natural or man-made. Without being given any information about the source of the material, their reply contained detailed data about the mineral composition and the following conclusion: "From the analysis it is impossible to state definitely, but from the appearance and nature of the samples, we are of the opinion that it is a cement which has been worked by man."

The small piece of parchment and other cleanings from the auger were taken by Putnam to Amherst, where many of the principal shareholders lived. Over thirty men were present in the Amherst court house on September 6, 1897, when Dr. A.E. Porter, a local physician, examined the material under a strong magnifying glass. He slowly and carefully flattened out the tiny ball-like piece of

Drawing of the piece of parchment found in the Treasure Pit in 1897.

parchment and to his surprise saw that it had writing on it in black ink. All that could be discerned were the letters *vi* or *wi*. These were later examined by writing experts in Boston and confirmed to have been written by a quill pen in India ink.

Here was tangible proof that something unusual and presumably valuable lay concealed in a man-made vault which had been carefully entombed in the depths of Oak Island. In a later interview with the *Toronto Telegraph*, Frederick Blair, who was to devote most of his life and resources to solving the mystery, and who was a brother Mason to the other members from Amherst, had this to say about the small piece of parchment: "That is more convincing evidence of buried treasure than a few doubloons would be. I am satisfied that either a treasure of immense value or priceless historical documents are in a chest at the bottom of the Pit."

In the light of these exciting discoveries, and with success seemingly in sight, the investors decided to refinance the operation using their own money rather than sell additional shares. Plans were quickly made for the resumption of work on the island. Because another flood tunnel was likely coming in from the south shore, it was agreed that the best plan was to sink a wide and deep shaft forty feet south of the original Pit and hope a single tunnel would cause the water in the Pit to drain into it. During the next six months, while pumps held the water in the Pit at the seventy-foot level, a total of six such shafts were dug in futile attempts to get at the treasure. All had to be abandoned because of unsafe working conditions, flooding from the sea or equipment malfunctions.

At this juncture, tests were carried out to confirm the existence of a south shore flood tunnel. Muddy water was pumped into the Pit above tide level and allowed to run out. The muddy water showed up along the south shore at about the low water mark at three separate locations. Red dye was then added to the water in the Pit and it also showed up in the water off the south shore. It was now obvious that a flooding system similar to the one found under the beach in Smith's Cove was present on the southern side of the island.

More encouraged than disheartened by this confirmation, which indicated to them that the treasure must be of incredible value, the company decided to make a final assault on the treasure pit. Starting in October 1899, the Pit was enlarged and a well-cribbed shaft measuring eight by ten feet was sunk. After clearing the Pit of piles of old lumber from other collapsed shafts, the men managed to reach the 113-foot level. All seemed to be going well, when suddenly all hopes of reaching the vault were dashed by seawater bursting in from two channels. Efforts were made to block off the water at source, but these ended in failure. And other problems added to the companies difficulties. Coal for the boiler driving the pumps and manual help were in short supply—many of the local men were involved in the more lucrative fishing industry. Final boring operations were inconclusive, and in the face of mounting debts, which forced a sheriff's auction of the company's machinery, there was no option but to suspend operations. Putman alone had lost over $20,000.

More than one hundred years had now passed since young Daniel McGinnis had stumbled upon the treasure pit. When he and his two companions had excitedly shovelled out the first few feet of dirt from the Pit, they would have had no way of knowing what their exciting discovery would lead to. During the intervening years, two men had been killed, hundreds of thousands of dollars had been spent, and twenty shafts and numerous tunnels had been dug in futile attempts to retrieve the mysterious treasure. Despite the plans of experienced engineers, the diligent attention of prudent businessmen and the backbreaking toil of countless individuals, the goal remained as elusive as ever. However, the labours of the past hundred years had produced indisputable evidence that sometime in the past a large group of men had constructed major underground workings on Oak Island for the purpose of installing and protecting something of presumably great value.

In spite of the astonishing discoveries of the previous few years, most of the investors were reluctant to carry on; businesses and families had suffered as a result of involvement in the Oak Island treasure search. Yet there was also a reluctance to allow new financial interests to take over. Finally a solution was found. By December 1900 all the investors of the Oak Island Treasure Company had sold their shares to one of their own. The challenge of retrieving the treasure now rested in the hands of a single individual, the eternal optimist, Frederick L. Blair. His conviction that a significant treasure was buried on Oak Island and his confidence that it would eventually be recovered were reflected in a letter he had written sometime earlier:

> When we went to work at the island two years ago, we knew comparatively nothing about conditions as they existed. We supposed at that time that the Money Pit was not over 120 feet deep and that the treasure was not over 110 feet down. Our work since has proved that the Pit is not less than 180 feet deep, that there are two tunnels instead of one, and that one of them is not less than 160 feet down, and that there is treasure at different levels in the Pit, from 126 feet down to 170 feet, without a doubt. . . . We now claim that there is nothing that can prevent us getting the treasure, if we succeed in getting a pumping pit down.

One wonders what powerful motive other than acquisition of material wealth led Blair, an intelligent, sober and religious-minded individual, to spend the remaining fifty years of his life trying to locate it.

7

Another Century Begins

Early in 1909, Henry Bowdoin, another New York–based engineer with impressive credentials, made the boastful claim that, with the help of a few local men, his own experience in mining and dredging combined with the use of modern machinery and engineering science would turn the Oak Island treasure hunt into little more than a two-week vacation. However, by May 1909, according to an interview printed in the New York *Sun*, he had realized that it was too big a job to tackle without selling a little stock first, and so he had set up the Old Gold Salvage and Wrecking Company, with head offices at 44 Broadway. It had authorized capital of $250,000 and offered shares to the general public at one dollar each. Frederick Blair and Captain John Welling were opted onto the board of directors and their presence was used to attract others to the venture. The company's prospectus compiled with their help provided a mini-historical review of the treasure search up to that time and made some grandiose claims:

> Over one hundred years ago a treasure, estimated to be over ten million dollars, was buried on Oak Island, in Mahone Bay, Nova Scotia, supposedly by pirates, who took such pains to safeguard it that, although numerous attempts have been made to recover it, it lies undisturbed to this day. These failures were due to lack of modern machinery and ignorance; each expedition being stopped by water and lack of funds. The pirates connected the pit in which the treasure was buried with the ocean by an underground tunnel, so that when buried and the tunnel opened the water level was sixty feet above the treasure. The diggers in the pit, which is quite a distance from the shore, have invariably been driven out by this water, which is salt, and rises and falls with the tide. As a pit was dug near the money pit one hundred and ten feet deep without striking any water, yet became flooded when they tunnelled

into the treasure pit, it proves the existence of an underground connection between the pit and the ocean. The location of this tunnel has been practically determined, but as yet no one has known how to cut it off.

That there is really some sort of treasure there has long been verified by gold shavings and part of a watch chain brought up with borings from the crude implements used. Since these borings were made, the parties have made regular payments on a lease of the property, which gives them the exclusive right to any treasure that may be found, which lease has been further augmented by a Government permit.

Believing, from the above, and from other facts, that a treasure of some value is buried in the pit on Oak Island, Nova Scotia, and knowing that with modern methods of machinery, the recovery of that treasure is easy, ridiculously easy, an exclusive contract has been entered into with the owners and leaseholders of the property for its recovery.

The prospectus then went on to outline in some detail the various methods that could be employed to recover the treasure which Bowdoin had estimated to be worth over $10 million. He promised a return of 4,000 per cent on each one-dollar share, with a minimum purchase of ten shares required. In addition, Bowdoin claimed that he had been informed of other hidden and sunken treasure sites elsewhere in the world that his Old Gold Salvage and Wrecking Company would later go after to the benefit of investors. Bowdoin's sweeping claims sounded too good to be true, and that is perhaps why he failed to attract as much investment as he was eventually to need. He had clearly set himself up for a steep fall. However, Franklin D. Roosevelt and some of his friends took the hook. They had little at stake and it was an affordable adventure if nothing else.

At this time, Henry Sellers still owned the eastern end of Oak Island which Frederick Blair rented from him for $100 per annum. Blair also held a forty-year mining lease and a "Treasure Trove" license from the government of Nova Scotia, which in return was to get a two per cent share of any valuables found. These agreements gave Blair exclusive and extensive rights over the treasure search, rights he used to attract men with experience and financing necessary for the project. Bowdoin seemed well qualified for the task at hand, although he did not manage to sell all the shares offered and had only enough backers for the short-term project he envisioned when he arrived on the island in August 1909. Roosevelt and the others involved arrived later.

Bowdoin was convinced he was about to get his hands on a cache of Captain Kidd's famous treasure and so he named his headquarters on the island "Camp Kidd" and inscribed a stone to that effect. Ignoring his stated intention of trying to block off the flood tunnel, he tackled the treasure pit head on. He found it just as the explorers of 1899 had left it, a five by seven foot shaft heavily cribbed to 110 feet and floored over at the thirty-foot water level. Bowdoin ordered it opened up and pumped out. On examining the shaft, the workmen found platforms every ten feet down connected by ladders. These were removed and the cribbing was strengthened. A diver was sent down to examine the watery depths of the Pit, and he reported that the wooden supports were in bad shape and planks were sticking up in all directions, making it impossible to proceed any further with the excavation. After managing to clear out the Pit to 113 feet, Bowdoin resorted to drilling.

After going through sixteen feet of gravel and sand, then another sixteen feet of blue clay mixed with small stones and sand, the drill hit cement at around 150 feet, just where they expected to find it. The core was six inches thick and they believed they had entered the vault and were about to drill into the treasure itself. However, all they found was another eighteen feet of yellow clay and stones down to bedrock at 167 feet. In all, twenty-five other drillholes were made to approximately the same depth, but apart from a small, thin disc of shiny metal that one of the workers later claimed to have seen on the core drill, nothing unusual was brought to the surface. Bowdoin sent samples of the cement-like material to Columbia University where it was submitted to tests and reported to be natural limestone pitted by the action of water. Another report released by one member of the company stated the material was rock-like and apparently man-made.

When November arrived with nothing to show for all his boasting, Bowdoin abandoned the island with the stated intention of returning the following summer of 1910 after Blair agreed to give him another try. However, later, writing from England, he tried to persuade Blair to give him access to the island until at least January 1, 1912. Sensing that something was amiss, Blair insisted that Bowdoin first provide proof of additional financial backing, something Bowdoin was unable to do.

In an attempt to force Blair's hand, the frustrated captain could not restrain himself from making the following written threat:

> I believe you had better see us if you come to New York this winter. Advise me ahead. If, however, we cannot get together on the time extension, it will be necessary for me to go to Oak Island and sell the machinery, etc., and when finished, the company will want a full report which one of our people, a newspaper man, will want to publish. The report that I would have to give them would not help in getting further investments in Oak Island.

Blair's reply was consistent with his steady temperament, his knowledge of Oak Island and his cool-headed assessment of the situation:

> Your letter almost conveys a threat that if we do not permit you to make further tests at Oak Island you will publish such information as would probably prevent the possibility of raising funds for exploration there in the future. Let me say that anything that can be said against Oak Island has already been written, and the publication of any article that you might be able to bring forth would not in the least jar us who own the lease.

Bowdoin made good on his threat with a highly critical article in *Collier's* magazine in August 1911. In the piece written by himself and entitled "Solving the Mystery of Oak Island," he claimed that, as far as he was concerned, there never was a treasure of any kind on Oak Island. He went on to debunk the idea of a man-made flood tunnel running inland from Smith's Cove and suggested that the salt water that continually filled the Pit percolated through the soil from the bay on the south shore of the island. He also refuted the claims that a ringbolt had been found embedded in a large rock on the beach or that a piece of chain, gold or otherwise, had been brought to the surface by earlier drilling.

Blair had been too long involved with Oak Island to let someone of Bowdoin's character and temperament have the last word. He replied to Bowdoin's charges by way of an article of his own in the Amherst "Daily News" on February 23, 1912. He stated that Bowdoin had refused or ignored advice from himself and others knowledgeable about the workings on Oak Island, and that he had done little exploratory work before resorting to dynamite, and thereby destroying the lower end of the Pit and causing it to go out of alignment. Concerning the cement, Blair referred to the previous tests carried out by A. Boake Roberts and Company of England. Blair dealt in turn with each of the issues raised by Bowdoin and made convincing arguments to the contrary and demonstrated how Bowdoin had dismissed incontrovertible evidence that the island had been worked on hundreds of years earlier and used to conceal and protect a treasure of some kind.

Undaunted by Bowdoin's failure on Oak Island and the adverse publicity, various other qualified but underfinanced individuals readily stepped forward during the next ten years to claim they had the means to recover the treasure, the value of which had surprisingly grown in proportion to the number of failures to retrieve it. As had happened during the previous hundred years, the new century was producing a steady stream of treasure hunters, all convinced they could succeed where others had failed.

Little major work was carried out on Oak Island in the years surrounding the First World War. In 1922, Blair, frustrated by several additional failures hastened by lack of sufficient capital, decided to advertize widely for someone with sufficient backing to carry on the search. He had to wait until 1931 before he finally found the man he was looking for, and he turned out to be someone who had been involved with Blair in his first attempt to find the treasure back in 1894.

William Chappell was one of four brothers who ran a successful lumber business throughout Nova Scotia. He had been present when the piece of parchment had been found and claimed he had seen traces of gold on the bit at the time. He was willing to try again, this time along with his brother Renwick and his son Melbourne, an engineer. Blair was hired by the company and lived on the island as field manager.

In spite of difficulties with the large water pump and accidents on the site, the main shaft was opened up to a depth of over 160 feet. Test drillings from that level indicated the presence of more cement-like material to a depth of twelve feet, then an empty space of about two feet, below which there was solid material of some kind. Optimistic that they were close to finding the treasure at last, the group vacated the island in October with the intention of returning the following spring. However, this plan was not to be.

The Chappells had already spent in excess of $30,000 with nothing to show for it. Economic conditions in Nova Scotia, as elsewhere, were becoming very shaky at the time, and to add to their uncertainty, the heirs of Sophia Sellers, who had died in the fall of 1931, refused to renew Blair's lease when it expired. There seems to have been some friction between the parties, and it was likely that the Sellers heirs were interested in a better deal. The Oak Island secret remained intact. For the next few years Blair had to watch from the sidelines as others tried and failed to find the treasure.

In spite of the problem that plagued his involvement with the Oak Island project, Blair remained as confident as ever of final success, as indicated in a letter written to an interested party at the time: "I have been connected with it for over thirty-eight years, have investigated it from all angles, and have gathered together a large amount of data on the subject and I am thoroughly convinced that a vast treasure lies buried there, and that modern engineering skill and appliances can easily recover it."

In 1934 he was joined by a man who not only shared his optimism but also had the money to put it to work.

8

Triangles, Treasure Maps and Tragedy

Gilbert Hedden had first read about the Oak Island mystery in the *New York Times* in 1928 while vice-president and general manager of the family business, Hedden Iron Construction Company of Hillside, New Jersey. The company was sold to the Bethlehem Steel Company in 1931, and Hedden remained on for another year as plant manager. His other business interests included insurance and an automobile dealership in Morristown, New Jersey. Hedden, a Freemason, was also interested in politics and served as mayor of Chatham, New Jersey, from 1934 to 1938.

With a large amount of capital to spare and an engineering background, Hedden was confident he could overcome the problems that had plagued others on Oak Island. Freeing himself of his business obligations, he came to Nova Scotia in 1934 and carried out extensive research into the history of the search from day one. He examined records of the earlier digs and interviewed previous explorers, including William Chappell. After visiting the island, he formed the opinion that there was a treasure hidden there and it was worth going after.

Blair was duly impressed with Hedden's credentials and most of all by the fact that he offered to sink up to $100,000 into a well-organized and professionally managed search. It seemed to be the perfect scenario for a final solution to the Oak Island mystery. However, an unforeseen problem soon arose from an unexpected source.

Blair had held the lease on the property for more than thirty years until the death of Sophia Sellers, the owner of the east end of the island, in 1931. He also held a Treasure Trove license, issued under the province's Mines Act, that was valid until 1944. One condition of this license at the time was that it could only be activated with the prior permission of the property owner. However, the Sellers heirs refused to renew the lease with Blair and instead offered to sell him

Part of an engraved rock found at Joudrey's Cove by G. Hedden in 1936.

the property in question for $5,000. Blair refused to pay what he considered to be an inflated price and so Hedden's plans were stalled.

After Blair had made an unsuccessful attempt through an associate in the Nova Scotia legislature to have the province's Mines Act amended to permit right of access by a license holder, Hedden purchased the entire east end of the island for the $5,000 in July 1935. He and Blair then entered into an agreement, and work finally got under way in June 1936 when the engineering firm of Sprague and Henwood of Scranton, Pennsylvania, arrived once again on the island. This time, a one-thousand-gallon-per-minute electric pump was used to dewater shaft number 21, sunk during the Chappell operation. The shaft was retimbered and extended to 170 feet, deeper than anyone had reached before. However, by fall nothing new had been discovered, and the company decided to wait until the following spring before sinking a new and much wider shaft nearby to facilitate lateral tunnelling.

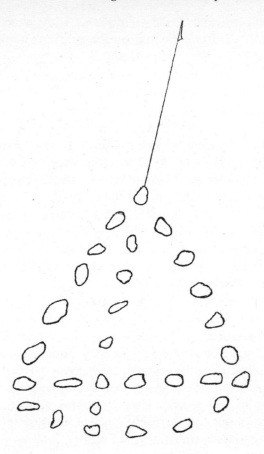

A ten foot equilateral triangle found on South Shore. First discovered in 1897 and rediscovered by G. Hedden in 1937.

During his first summer on Oak Island, Hedden spent many hours exploring the beaches and terrain for traces of anything that would help him in his search. His curiosity was rewarded when he noticed the ends of two large timbers protruding about four feet apart from the rocks inside the remains of the coffer dam built at Smith's Cove in 1866. When removed from under four feet of sand, they both were found to be fifteen inches in diameter and notched every four feet, each notch containing wooden pins. Several wooden cross members, about four feet long, were also found. They were believed at the time to have been part of a skid used much earlier on the island. The discovery of other large timbers in the area in the

1970s would confirm that they were part of a larger structure, possibly the coffer dam constructed by the original workers on Oak Island.

That summer Hedden also came across several pieces of marked rock on the island's north shore, some of which were buried several feet below the surface of the beach at Joudrey's Cove. The most interesting and largest piece contained symbols which, although unusual to the average observer, may well have been understood by Hedden, a well-educated and dedicated Freemason. Of a sacred nature, they included the Masonic sign for the Creator, a circle with a central dot, and the Christian symbol of the Cross.

In May 1937, shaft number 22, later referred to as the Hedden shaft, was put down just east of the Chappell shaft. Measuring twelve by twenty-four feet, it was the largest ever opened on the island and is the one shaft in the Pit area still visible today. Not surprisingly, it cut into an earlier shaft not too far below the surface. Remnants of much earlier work such as heavy drill casings and a miner's whale-oil lamp were uncovered less than fifty feet further down. At ninety-three feet workers found the remains of a collapsed flood tunnel and a band of putty-like clay similar to that found during earlier excavations. By August, drilling had reached 160 feet and pieces of oak had been bought to the surface, leading to the conviction that the missing wooden chests had been located. However, at this point Hedden surprisingly stopped work on the shaft and focused his attention elsewhere.

The object of his attention was a treasure map in a book entitled *Captain Kidd and his Skeleton Island*, by Harold T. Wilkins, which had been published in England earlier that year. Reginald Harris had brought the book to Hedden's attention because its author claimed that the map, which had some similarities to Oak Island, was authentic and had belonged to Captain William Kidd. The map had no nautical bearings and all indications were that the island lay in a tropical region far removed from Nova Scotia. However, Hedden managed to find enough similarities to be convinced that there was a connection and began to look for markers that would tie in with measurements given on the Kidd map.

Blair then informed Hedden of the discovery of a large equilateral stone triangle on the south shore by himself and Captain Welling in 1897. Hedden immediately cleared out the spot on the grassy bank just above the high water mark and found the triangle still intact. Its sides were each ten feet in length and made up of large, round beach stones about the size of a man's head. A curved line of similar-sized stones extended about three feet below the base line joining both ends. Another straight line connected this with the apex of the triangle and pointed true north in the direction of the Pole Star. When extended, this line crossed close to the location of the original Pit. To some observers at the time, the stone structure resembled a large sextant. Blair and Hedden, both Masons, must have pondered on the possible symbolic meaning of this equilateral triangle, a geometric form commonly used in Masonic literature and lore. Hedden decided to investigate its significance in relation to the Kidd map, and his interest was further fuelled by Blair's disclosure that a large, drilled granite rock had also been found in 1895 some fifty feet north of the treasure pit.

Hedden initiated a search and a second drilled rock was found due east of the first near the shoreline at Smith's Cove. The holes in both rocks were definitely man-made, and each was two inches deep by one and a quarter inches wide. What was most significant to Hedden was that the measurements between these items were with one notable exception closely similar to the measurements between the markers drawn on the Kidd map. Hedden then had these verified by Charles Roper, a Halifax land surveyor.

Convinced in his own mind that the map in the book referred to Oak Island, Hedden even informed President Roosevelt of his startling discovery and received a cordial but noncommittal reply. He also corresponded with the author, Harold Wilkins, who in turn tried to assure Hedden that there was no connection whatsoever. Undaunted, Hedden cancelled further work on the island and travelled to England to meet and talk with Wilkins. The whole matter was resolved when Wilkins admitted that the map was a compilation of four shown to him by antique dealer Hubert Palmer and of others he had seen in the British Museum. Wilkins told Hedden that the island represented on the map was likely in the China Sea. Hedden's insistence that there really was a similarity with Oak Island led Wilkins to believe that Hedden could possibly be the reincarnation of Captain Kidd and that he himself was destined to help recover the treasure.

At this point Hedden had seen and heard enough to begin to doubt Wilkins' sanity. After meeting with Palmer and viewing the four supposedly authentic charts, each of which were different,

Hedden gave up his quest. However, he held onto the belief that Kidd, who sailed out of New York, may have somehow known about the treasure deposit on Oak Island. If nothing else, the whole affair had led to the rediscovery of the stone triangle and the drilled stones which many people feel bear some relationship to the location of the treasure.

Instead of returning to Oak Island to continue the search, Hedden returned to his home in New Jersey. Once more the jinx that had plagued successive Oak Island treasure hunters was about to strike. Unknown to Blair and Chappell, Hedden was heading for a financial crisis. He had already spent thousands of dollars on the venture and was running into income tax problems at home. In March 1938 he was forced to withdraw from any further investment or activity on Oak Island. Blair was deeply disappointed by Hedden's sudden withdrawal and noted in a letter to his lawyer, Harris, that he felt betrayed, especially by a brother Mason. However, because he had put his property in a trust, Hedden was able to hold onto it and retained an interest in the treasure search.

Next up to bat was yet another New York engineer. In fact, Edwin Hamilton was an associate professor of Engineering at New York University and a high-ranking member of the city's Masonic community. After working out a mutually agreeable arrangement with Hedden, who owned the property, and Blair, who held the Treasure Trove license, he arrived on the island in 1938, leased Hedden's machinery, hired a gang of local men and spent six years at the plate trying to hit the Oak Island home run.

By 1943 he had spent in excess of $60,000 without finding any treasure. But his extensive work on the island had established for the first time the existence of man-made tunnels below the bedrock at 200 feet and revealed an even more extensive flooding system on the island's south shore.

In the summer of 1943, Hamilton covered up the exposed shafts and headed back home after expressing his belief, based on his own observations, that something of great value must have been buried on the island. He later "retired" to Chester where he set up a boat-building business.

Hamilton's involvement with Oak Island is also notable because he corresponded with President Roosevelt about his progress with the treasure search. The American president even planned to visit the island during his tenure, but the war in Europe intervened.

In May 1950, anxious to recoup some of his losses and get out of a difficult working relationship with Blair, Hedden finally relieved himself of the property when John Whitney Lewis, an elderly New York mining engineer with many years of experience in the field, made an offer of $6,000. Hedden also told Lewis that Blair's Treasure Trove license had expired, which it had at the time.

Unfortunately for Lewis, his license application was turned down by the province on the grounds that a license had already been reissued to Frederick Blair, who had acted promptly after hearing of the sale to Lewis. For a time neither could move, but the stalemate was finally broken when the Nova Scotia legislature, after lobbying by Blair and Melbourne Chappell, conveniently passed an amendment to the Treasure Trove Act in 1950 which gave the holder of such a licence legal access to property owned by another party. This put Blair and Chappell, who had already agreed to carry on the search, firmly in the driver's seat. Left out in the cold by this adroit Bluenose political manoeuvring, Lewis chose to sell the property at cost to a more than grateful Mel Chappell.

Within six months of this transaction, Blair was dead, the license was transferred and for the first time the land and the Treasure Trove licence were in the hands of a single individual—Mel Chappell of Sydney, the former Grand Master of all Nova Scotia Masons—who would remain a major player in the Oak Island treasure search for the next thirty years. His sons Douglas and Norman Chappell maintained the family's connection to and interest in the mystery into the 1990s.

Chappell's sharp business sense seemed to fail him when he took over the Oak Island operation. During the next few years he lost $30,000 in various futile experiments with a gold-finding machine designed by Welsford Parker of Belleville, Ontario. From then on he decided to let someone else finance the search.

That opportunity came in 1955 in the form of a Stetson-hatted and cigar-chewing oil drilling engineer from Texas with money to burn: George Greene. His confident Texan talk of quickly finding the treasure was backed by many years of experience in the field, the bankroll of several oil company executives and the fact that his uncle John Shields had been associated with Franklin D. Roosevelt during the Bowdoin project of 1909.

Greene carried out an extensive drilling program in the area around the Pit. Other than locating a large cavern below the 110-foot level and fuelling speculation about a natural cavity in the bedrock, Green's tenure on Oak Island produced little new evidence. By October he was back in Texas and, in spite of his earlier claims, he never returned. It is with good reason that Canada's national engineering journal once described Oak Island as an embarrassment to the whole engineering community.

By this time the treasure hunt had been going on for 169 years. Numerous shafts had been sunk on the eastern end of the island in various attempts to locate the treasure. Many tunnels now existed at various levels below the surface, and water was flowing in and out with tremendous force through a maze of channels. The Oak Island mystery was now far from a romantic adventure: it had become a technically difficult, time-consuming and financially demanding puzzle. It was also a dangerous one: two men had already lost their lives and several had been injured. There had been all kinds, perhaps an unusually high number, of unfortunate problems with machinery and material over the years. Oak Island had shown the world that, in spite of the seductive lure it exerted on men's minds, it could not easily be conquered. It was more than a demanding mistress; it had become a merciless and unforgiving taskmaster to the unwary, unskilled and unprepared, as was soon to be tragically demonstrated.

After Greene's unexpected departure, Chappell had no trouble finding yet another eager-beaver treasure hunter. Robert Restall was a former daredevil motorcyclist who had been waiting in the wings for five years for his chance to win the prize. Restall and his wife Mildred had challenged fate many times before in their *Globe of Death* carnival routine, during which they had crisscrossed each other on motorcycles at tremendous speeds inside an iron cage. When they set up their home with their two boys near the Pit on placid-looking Oak Island in 1960, they never thought they were embarking on something far more dangerous than anything they had ever faced before.

During his early days on the island, Restall spent time exploring and found three huge piles of stones forming a triangle on the hillside northwest of the treasure pit. He also dug up a stone slab from under the sand at Smith's Cove with the date "1704" carved into it. Convinced that pirates from LaHave had buried their loot on Oak Island, he succeeded in raising sufficient backing for himself and his family to live frugally on the island while carrying out a bare-bones search for a treasure he was sure would make him a multimillion-

aire. Doing much of the laborious work by hand, helped by his eigh-
teen-year-old son Robert, Restall first concentrated his efforts on the
Hedden shaft. Progress was slow and not very rewarding.

Realizing that he needed to stop the water flow if he hoped to
reach the treasure, he sunk a twenty-five by ten foot shaft close to
the estimated entrance of the flooding system at Smith's Cove. On
an hot and humid August afternoon in 1965, Restall, Robert, Karl
Graeser, one of Restall's backers from New York, and Cyril Hiltz, a
teenager from nearby Martin's Point who had been helping out were
overcome by either methane gas or fumes emitted by the gasoline-
driven motor attached to a water pump at the head of the shaft and
they all drowned in the shallow water at the bottom of the pit.

The Oak Island treasure hunt had now cost six men their lives
and brought grief and hardship to their families. Hundreds of thousands of dollars had been spent in the 170-year-long search, leaving
some well-to-do businessmen nearly penniless and struggling to
recover their losses. Several experienced engineers had ended up
more than a little perplexed by the island's persistent refusal to
reveal its secret, and every attempt had been fraught with unforeseen
problems of one kind or another.

Much of the east end of the island had been dug into, tunnelled
through, drilled and dynamited, but no one had been able to outsmart
the designer of the intricate underground workings. To some
observers it seemed as if an invisible force was protecting the treasure. Of course, the whole business of retrieving it had been made
all the more difficult and complicated when the early excavators had
tripped the water traps and caused the Pit to flood and the platform
holding the chests to collapse into the depths. In view of all these
factors, it was almost astonishing that anyone would want to continue with the project, but not even the recent four deaths on the island
proved deterrent enough to others lured by a fabulous buried treasure and convinced of their own ability to find it.

9

War on Oak Island

Some men are destined to leave a physical mark on their surroundings, and Robert Dunfield was such a man. This petroleum geologist from California's high-powered and highly mechanized approach to finding the treasure stood out in stark contrast to Restall's pick-and-shovel operation and left many people distraught by the thoughtless destruction of some of Oak Island's archaeologically important landscape, stone markings and underground workings.

Dunfield had visited the island during Restall's tenure and felt confident that money and modern machinery was all that was needed to solve the mystery once and for all. He had the backing of several West Coast businessmen, and Dan Blankenship of Florida also invested in the venture. Having cut a quick deal with Chappell soon after Restall's death, Dunfield proposed the construction of a causeway to the island. Chappell, who had some good political contacts, received speedy approval, and almost within weeks a 650-foot-long causeway was built across Crown waters to facilitate the movement of Dunfield's heavy machinery onto the island.

Sure that the operation would take up no more than three weeks of his valuable time, at a total expenditure of less than $50,000, he began his assault in October 1965. At first convinced that the operation was to be little more than an exercise in open-pit mining and water control, Dunfield set his bulldozers to work skimming at least ten feet of surface soil off a large area surrounding the Pit and moving tons of earth onto the beach at Smith's Cove. He managed to expose the cribbing of the original Pit but failed to stop water from entering it. Dunfield then arranged for a seventy-foot-high clamdigger and pumping equipment capable of handling 110,000 gallons an hour to be set up at the site. The massive machinery and two dozen men in two crews ended up creating a crater 50 feet wide and some 150 feet deep, but broken porcelain, rusted drill casings and old timbers were all they found.

By December Dunfield was still there, as certain as ever that within days he would expose the treasure. But nature and those mischievous Oak Island gremlins intervened once again. Over the Christmas holidays heavy rains caused a mud slide that made the crater unworkable, and a second crane brought in to replace the first one soon had a cracked engine block. Then there were instances of what Chappell later implied was sabotage. Dunfield's heavy-handed tactics had apparently not been popular locally. Determined to carry on, even though it was costing by his own estimation about $2,000 a day, Dunfield started off the new year by having the opening filled in and beginning all over again, this time with the intention of excavating a crater 100 feet wide and 180 feet deep if necessary. Once solid ground had been restored, a drilling rig was set up. One drill entered a cavity below bedrock at 140 feet; its bit went through the limestone bedrock, then through a two-foot wooden roof and into a forty-five-foot-high chamber, at the bottom of which it struck metal of some kind. Dunfield was sure he had relocated the underground chamber found by Greene and others.

In an all-out effort to block off the seawater, Dunfield had his men and heavy machinery excavate an elongated tunnel along the south shore, destroying the stone triangle and who knows what else in the process. The opening, fifty feet long by twenty feet wide, exposed an eight-foot-square original shaft below the triangle but failed to stop the flooding in the Pit. Dunfield then put his massive digger to work at Smith's Cove to destroy any remnants of the finger-like drains. He also used the digger to open up the "Cave-in Pit" and, finding nothing there, left it a water-filled open crater. By March 1966, having spent nearly $150,000 with no tangible results, the once highly confident Dunfield was by now showing the strain. No doubt some of his backers were also uneasy. He returned or was called back to California "until the weather gets better," and although he promised to return "to finish the job," his brash and highly destructive attempt to solve the Oak Island mystery had run its course. His departure also resulted in some measure from the facts that both a new participant and a new problem had been added to the already challenging treasure hunt.

Frederick Nolan, a Bedford, Nova Scotia, surveyor, had first become interested in Oak Island in the late 1950s. He had visited the island then being worked on by Texan George Greene and later spent many hours in conversation with author Reginald Harris. By that time, Harris, the Grand Historian for Nova Scotia Freemasonry, had also become the unofficial historian of the Oak Island mystery and had accumulated quite a collection of papers, letters, maps, clippings and legal documents on the subject. Having been both Blair and Chappell's lawyer and the legal agent for members of various other search parties, he had an intimate knowledge of who and what had been involved with Oak Island over the years. Nolan was impressed with Harris's accumulated knowledge and became convinced that an extraordinary treasure still lay buried on the island.

As a young professional surveyor, Nolan was fascinated by the various carved stones and stone markers that had been reportedly found on the island. He was convinced that in some way they related to the location and mode of recovery of the treasure. Anxious to put his expertise to work, he had approached Mel Chappell, owner of the property at the time. However, Robert Restall had already been in line to mine the riches of Oak Island, and so Nolan's request was refused. But being keen to get working, and with his knowledge of surveying at his fingertips, Nolan convinced Chappell to allow him to carry out an extensive survey of the island's stone markers before any further damage might be done to them. As he later admitted, he was already convinced there was more to Oak Island than the so-called "Money Pit." Although Charles Roper, the province's land surveyor, had carried out a survey for Hedden back in 1937, it had concentrated solely on a specific area on the island's eastern end. Nolan had more ambitious plan.

By 1962 Nolan had completed a comprehensive survey of the whole island at thousands of dollars of his own expense, during which he placed almost two dozen bronze markers in concrete blocks he poured in the ground. In the process, he cut and walked dozens of lines through the evergreen bush and took notes on the positions of various stone structures, such as the equilateral triangle on the south shore and the triangles formed by four large old piles of stones on top of the island's highest hill. Comparing these and other markers to the survey grid of the whole island, he became certain that an extensive, well-thought-out and much more complicated plan than previously imagined had been used to bury and record the position of the treasure. In fact, Nolan came to the conclusion that there were several treasure sites on the island, some of which had already been located. As soon as his survey work was complete, he approached Chappell with the results in the hope of being given the opportunity to excavate in the Pit area. Chappell already had Restall digging at that site and was allowing a Vancouverite by the name of

Laverne Johnson to test out his own theory in relation to another site to the northeast. Chappell, on the lookout for a well-backed operator for his next partner, consistently refused to consider Nolan's persistent requests. In his eagerness, Nolan eventually irked Chappell, who turned around and told him to "go to hell."

Frustrated, and suspicious about Chappell's claim to ownership of the entire island, Nolan went to the Chester municipal office in 1963 and meticulously checked into the details of the property title. He was naturally delighted to discover that the deed of sale between Whitney Lewis and Chappell in 1950 had not included seven lots in the centre of the island. He took note of the deed holders of these lots, heirs of Sophia Sellers, and quietly approached them. Because the lots, numbered five, and nine through fourteen, were with one exception all in the central swampy part of the island, they were more than happy to sell for the $2,500 he offered. This quiet coup gave Nolan ownership of a strategically placed quarter of the 128-acre island.

Feeling he was now in a good bargaining position, Nolan reapproached Chappell, this time with an offer to trade his newly acquired lots for the chance to tackle the Pit. The somewhat flabbergasted Chappell was outraged by Nolan's wiliness. This was the beginning of an era of protracted disputes and intense discord between rival treasure searchers on Oak Island which has continued to this day.

Chappell, who claimed he had purchased the whole island from Lewis, was more than a little miffed at finding himself undermined in this way. He promptly instructed his lawyer Reginald Harris to clear up the matter. Legal correspondence between New York, Halifax and Chester followed and resulted in an outraged Chappell having to accept the fact that he now had to share Oak Island with the upstart surveyor from Bedford. Nolan later acquired his own Treasure Trove license and ever since there have been two official treasure hunts on Oak Island.

Until October 1965, when Dunfield built the causeway, all personnel and equipment had come by boat or barge to the island. Often they had unloaded at makeshift landing areas in Smith's or Joudrey's coves. Other times they had landed at the nearest point to the mainland on the island's western tip and followed a trail that ran eastwards through the centre of the island. For some unknown reason, this trail ended up in the swamp. Over time this trail had been widened and made to bypass the swamp by way of dry land on its north side; it climbed the hill on the northeast and then turned southwards to the Pit area. With the passage of years, men and machinery, what was once a trail had become a rough road. After the construction of the causeway, it was the established route from one end of the island to the other, even though it had passed through property not owned by the treasure hunters. Dunfield, like Chappell, resented Nolan's intrusion on the island and belligerently refused to allow him to use the causeway. In 1966 the Californian Dunfield even posted an armed guard to make sure he didn't. The Wild West had come east, and for the first time guns were used by treasure hunters on Oak Island. Not being one to walk away from a challenge, Nolan responded in his own quietly determined way. He bought a piece of property on the mainland at Crandall's Point immediately adjacent to the causeway and blocked off access to it. The two protagonists stared each other down until Dunfield for various reasons was forced to abandon the project. No doubt the ill will generated by this development had added to his mounting mechanical and financial problems and made him more than willing to high-tail it back to California.

10

The Oak Island Cross

From the time he had first examined Roper's survey and begun notating the various stone markers he found on the island, Frederick Nolan had been aware that there was probably more to the Oak Island mystery than had previously been considered.

While Dan Blankenship made plans to take over operations on the east end of the island after Dunfield's departure in 1966, Nolan proceeded to carry out exploration work on his own property and partly drained the swamp that straddled it.

During one of my early meetings with the slightly built but agile Nolan, the seventy-year-old treasure hunter told me that when first surveying the island he had come across four large stone piles on the northeastern hilltop. He described these piles as about twelve feet wide at the base and more than four feet high. During a later meeting in a Bedford restaurant, he drew a rough diagram on a serviette to demonstrate how the stone piles formed two distinct triangles, the larger of which pointed westward towards the swamp, the other northwest towards Joudrey's Cove. According to Nolan, the sides of the larger triangle were about 150 feet long, and the base was roughly 100 feet in length.

During the late 1960s and 1970s, Nolan found enough evidence to be convinced that whoever was responsible for the underground workings on the island had also left many remnants of their work on his property. He came across several drilled rocks and others that had primitive cement and metal ringbolts embedded in them. He also found a sizable heart-shaped stone and another which formed a large arrowhead. In addition, he discovered the remains of a very old well and smithy next to the swamp.

An avid surveyor, Nolan shot numerous transit lines between various stones and discovered still more unusual rocks at points of intersection or along sight lines. These included a number of upright, marked pieces of sandstone which Nolan was convinced had been purposely placed in position. One of the more notable of these was a narrow and pointed, eighteen-inch-high rectangular stone which

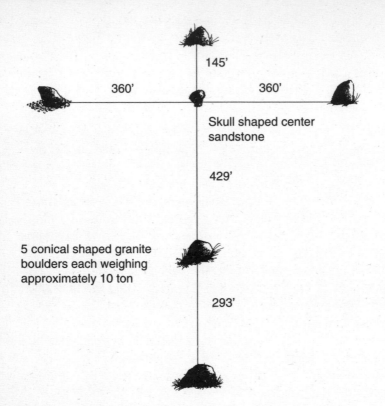

145'

360'   360'

Skull shaped center
sandstone

429'

5 conical shaped granite
boulders each weighing
approximately 10 ton

293'

Megalithic Cross discovered by F. Nolan in the early 1980s.

geologist Bob Grantham of the Nova Scotia Museum of Natural History intimated had man-worked characteristics, including chisel and burn marks.

While draining the swamp in 1970, Nolan also recovered some very old stakes and a piece of wood with a metal hinge still attached, which he believed may have been part of a chest. He also found what appeared to be a gold-bar branding iron, also very old. These and other discoveries in the swamp, such as a small piece of a wooden ship's gunwale, were later interpreted as indications that this low-lying area may have been used as a docking or boat-repair yard at one time.

Nolan, influenced by his experience as a professional surveyor, readily concluded that many of the unusual marked rocks and stone structures found on his property were really part of a massive man-made, grid-like map that contained a mysterious pattern that pointed to the hiding place of the main treasure. He also came to believe that the main treasure cache, one of several he thinks were buried on the island, lay on or close to his property. He spent many years trying to unravel this maze, but after various digs at different suspected locations he failed to find anything of value. Although perhaps some elements of sour grapes and blinkered thinking lay behind some of Nolan's initial conclusions, his discoveries in and around the swamp strongly indicate that the work carried out by those who deposited the treasure did extend beyond the immediate area of the Pit. Blankenship's many discoveries on the island, which include wire and a piece of solid metal at a depth of 100 feet in a shaft some 680 feet northeast of the Pit, have added weight to this hypothesis.

As a result of his exhaustive field research, Nolan realized, more than anyone before him, that distinctive geometric patterns and precise mathematical measurements had been used to position the various marked stones and stone markers. From what he observed on the ground, he concluded that a vast and well-organized enterprise had been carried out on the island by men with knowledge of mathematics and engineering. He also came to believe, as others have, that there must be another, less troublesome way to get at the treasure. In fact, Nolan feels the Pit was constructed as an elaborate decoy.

Laverne Johnson, a retired hospital engineer from Vancouver, who had carried out sporadic excavation work on the island in the early 1960s shares the same view but believes he and not Nolan has the right answer for the location of the treasure. Johnson adopted a more intelligent approach than most previous treasure hunters, and his precise calculations put the treasure in the high ground northwest of the Pit.

Nolan's thoughtful and patient approach, during which he actually crawled around on the uneven and overgrown terrain for countless hours in search of clues, coupled with his knowledge of surveying and his meticulous calculations produced many surprising and interesting results. It was while he was pursuing this line of investigation that he came across his largest and most dramatic discovery: a megalithic cross embedded in the ground.

First verified in 1981 but not revealed to the public until much later because, according to Nolan, of a protracted court case launched against him by the owners of the rest of the island in 1983, this extensive formation had all the earmarks of being man-made.

Comprised of five large, cone-shaped granite stones, each of which weighs approximately ten tons, the cross straddles a large section of Nolan's property and lies in a nearly northeast to southwest orientation. Four of the boulders are positioned to form the extremities of the body and arms of the cross, and there is an additional boulder about one-third the way up from the base.

A sixth stone, made of softer sandstone, was found under the ground exactly midway between the boulders forming the arms of the cross. This central rock had been worked by hand or been eroded by nature to give the appearance of a crude human head. This central boulder also has a well-defined groove, shaped like a dagger, on its sandstone face.

The measurements between this skull rock, as Nolan calls it, and the granite boulders at either end of the arms are exactly the same: 360 feet. The total length of the stem of the cross is 867 feet, and there are some close but not precise correlations between the structure's various internal measurements. The crossing lines between the arms and the body of the structure form four precise right angles.

Nolan's conclusion is that the cross is part of a geometric code constructed by military engineers to indicate the location of the real treasure, which he believes is part of the enormous wealth taken by the British after the sacking of Havana in 1762. He believes that a secret conclave of British military officers arranged to have some of this booty diverted to Oak Island while the rest was being shipped back to England.

The argument against this theory is that radiocarbon dating shows the work involved was carried out much earlier. In addition, by 1762 many settlers had arrived in Chester and the surrounding area, which would have made a secret and long, drawn-out project on Oak Island at the time almost impossible. However, when one considers that from the beginning of the seventienth century several senior British officials were Freemasons or Rosicrucians and the Masonic Order later permeated the whole military structure, Nolan's theory becomes more plausible.

Unfortunately for Nolan, soon after he had made the exciting discovery of the cross, his field research ended up in limbo for four years and his exploration work came to a temporary halt. In 1983 he found himself preoccupied, defending a serious court challenge to his ownership of part of the island. Members of a treasure-hunting syndicate had bought out Mel Chappell, and their relationship with Nolan had been quite fractious at times.

11

Chests, Tools, Timbers and Bones

During the sixteen years Nolan had been busy searching and excavating on his property, equally exciting discoveries were being made elsewhere on Oak Island.

In 1966 Dan Blankenship was so sure he could meet and beat the challenge presented by Oak Island that he was willing to spend additional time and effort on the project, even after his $20,000 investment in Dunfield's operation had disappeared with the tons of soil Dunfield had dumped in the ocean. However, he needed additional financing, so late in 1967 he teamed up with Montreal businessman David Tobias, who had first visited Oak Island while training with the RCAF at Maitland, Nova Scotia, during the Second World War. Tobias, like so many others before him, had become intrigued by the mystery, and he had eventually invested in Restall's operation. By the time of Dunfield's departure, Tobias had been keen to become more actively involved and found a capable and willing partner in the Florida contractor Blankenship.

After taking over the operation from Dunfield, the less bombastic but eager Blankenship offered Nolan $1,000 for six months of access to the causeway. Nolan was more than happy to declare a truce, and both parties proceeded with their own plans to find the treasure.

Tobias and his partner first tried to locate the second flood tunnel on the south shore, but their attempt was halted when part of the shaft they were working in, the twenty-eighth dug on the island, collapsed in on itself. But their excavations under the beach at Smith's Cove revealed items such as an old metal set-square, a handworked heart-shaped stone and a pair of iron scissors; the set-square and scissors were estimated by experts to be between two and three hundred years old.

Anxious to produce new proof that something had been buried on Oak Island, and with an eye to attracting additional investment,

Heart shaped stone found under the beach at Smith's Cove in 1967.

Tobias hired the Becker Drilling Company of Calgary to carry out a deep drilling program in the area surrounding the Pit. Huntec Limited, a seismic and geophysical testing company, was also hired. Tobias then called in consulting engineer Colin Campbell of Toronto, a man considered to be one of Canada's leading mining engineers and an historian of underground workings. After studying the reports of previous explorations on the island, visiting the site and examining the drilling results produced concurrently by the Becker Drilling Company of Calgary, his report to Tobias contained the following:

> The discovery in 1795 of a well defined pit 13' in diameter with a platform every 10' in depth to 30' indicated men had operated underground many years before. Subsequent searches underground and on surface were carried out at intermittent periods of varying lengths until your present operations. These operations established the following factors.
>
> (1) A large number of men were engaged for a few years driving various shafts, inclined and lateral headings, some of which were apparently prepared for flooding in order to discourage any inquisitive searchers.

(2) The Glacial till of the Island is underlain by blue clay and red marl and thence limestone, which in at least a considerable area, contains gypsum.

All previous searches have been confined to the horizons above the limestone and/or gypsum and, since several additional headings have been driven by the searchers, the area adjacent to the original Pit is in a most disturbed state and would require elaborate precautions to sink another shaft through it.

(4) The underlying rock (limestone and/or gypsum) seems to be stable enough to have headings driven into it and your recent drilling indicates there were some operations there. Since none of the searches reached this horizon then it is reasonable to assume that these operations were carried out by those who buried the treasure.

(5) Many of the searches were financed only for limited periods, hence the inconclusive results from their efforts, and abandonment of operations before reaching their objectives.

During recent months operations at Oak Island have been concentrated on drilling over forty holes. Several of these have reached depths of over 200 feet. The drilling has been done by the Becker Drilling Company of Calgary and has resulted in some additional information and more particularly about the horizon between 178' and 212' that was not previously known and has also confirmed some previous opinions regarding upper horizons. . . .

In my opinion the early operations by the `pirates' or other parties were too elaborate and well planned to be for any minor venture and therefore it is reasonable to assume that the operations were for the purpose of hiding treasure which must be of great value to warrant the effort.

The results of the various searches have confirmed that the horizons above the limestone and/or gypsum have been deliberately flooded by the `pirates' or other parties after the original operations were completed. The finding of cement would indicate they also sealed or attempted to seal the openings in the limestone and/or gypsum.

In my opinion, the search should be directed to the limestone and/or gypsum horizon below and adjacent to

the original pit and this can be accomplished most eco-
nomically by sinking a shaft where the ground is reason-
ably stable, probably about 100 feet from the original pit
and then explore the limestone and/or gypsum by diamond
drilling from lateral headings. . . .

I believe that a search at lower horizons than those previously investigated is warranted.

Tobias and Blankenship now had a convincing argument and
enough evidence to interest other investors in their plans to retrieve
the treasure, plans which would require solid and long-term financial backing. Triton Alliance Limited was officially formed in 1969
as a Montreal-based private company. Its primary purpose was to
dig for for treasure, but its promotional literature also claimed that
its interests extended to involvement in activities of an historical and
archaeological nature on Oak Island. According to the *Financial
Post* of March 21, 1970, the company comprised twenty-four
investors who, between them, were willing to gamble up to half a
million dollars in the hope of a sizable return. The article stated they
were "a largely unidentified group of some of Canada's wealthiest
and best known businessmen." Early shareholders in the company to
tackle the Oak Island mystery included the aging Melbourne
Chappell, who still owned most of the island; William Sobey, then
head of the Sobey supermarket empire; George Jennison, a past
president of the Toronto Stock Exchange; other bankers and
financiers; the politically minded lawyer Gordon Coles, who was
later to become Nova Scotia's deputy attorney general; and millionaire Boston land-developer Charles Brown III. In various media
reports about the formation of the company, Tobias expressed complete confidence in the future success of the venture, which for the
first time was being described as something more than a hunt for
buried gold. In a magazine article at the time, Tobias was quoted as
saying that the project was of great historical importance, having
added enigmatically that "we are the first people to know what to
expect and what we are after."

Becker Drilling's extensive work in the area of the treasure pit
had established the presence of previously undiscovered tunnels or
caverns below the island's bedrock at about 200 feet. After passing
through an extensive layer of solid limestone and gypsum, the drills
had cut through several inches of wood interspersed with a layer of

blue clay and then dropped through open space for up to ten feet before hitting solid bedrock again. Samples of wood and pieces of metal, cement and china had been brought to the surface. Radiocarbon dating of some of these specimens showed they were several hundred years old. Goechron Laboratories of Cambridge, Massachusetts were sent samples of the wood found below the bedrock. Their radiocarbon dating of one of the samples determined its age to correspond to the year 1575, plus or minus eighty-five years. The Steel Company of Canada examined the metal pieces and established that they were also several hundred years old. Canada Cement Lafarge identified the cement samples as of a primitive type common during the sixteenth and seventeenth centuries. These results and those supplied by the seismic readings led Blankenship and Tobias to a firm belief that they had located previously undiscovered natural and man-worked cavities below the bedrock.

With the formation of Triton and the inflow of additional capital, another attempt was made in 1970 to block off the flow of seawater from the eastern shore by building a massive coffer dam in Smith's Cove. This dam was bigger and further out in the water than the previous two had been, but it also soon fell victim to the unrelenting power of nature. However, during its short lifespan it led to the discovery of part of a large, semicircular wooden structure in the exposed seabed made up of huge logs, some two feet thick and as long as sixty feet, which were notched at four-foot intervals and had Roman numerals beside each notch. Several of the notches had wooden pegs slotted into holes drilled in the logs. Like the earlier discovery by Hedden, this structure was believed by experts, including geologist Dr. H. Cooke of Dalhousie University, to have been part of a dock or slipway and possibly part of the original coffer dam built by those who installed the flooding system. Wood taken from one of the logs was radiocarbon dated at Brock University in Ontario and it was found to be more than 250 years old. The National Research Council of Canada examined additional pieces of fibrous material found nearby under the beach by Blankenship and confirmed that it was coconut fibre. A sample of this same material found by Tobias was radiocarbon dated and to everyone's surprise was found to be much older than the wood samples.

Another interesting find made on the island's east end was a large granite stone with the letter G carved into it. The stone was uncovered by accident when men and machinery were backfilling the

"Cave-in Pit." The sharp-eyed Blankenship, ever on the lookout for anything unusual, noticed the cutting in the stone as it was pushed out of the ground on its way to the gaping, water-filled cavern. He moved quickly to retrieve it and examination convinced him this was no hoax left by a previous treasure hunter. The side on which the letter G was carved had been embedded in the ground and was quite clean, whereas a border of lichen had grown around the rock above the level where it jutted out of the ground. This stone is still on the island, resting at the bottom of the hill at Smith's Cove.

In 1970, Golder Associates of Toronto was contracted to carry out exhaustive underground tests by way of deep drilling and seismic soundings below bedrock on the island's east end. The results of this costly research again convinced Triton that a series of man-made and natural cavities were present at depths not previously explored.

Based on the exploratory drilling, geotechnical tests and Colin Campbell's recommendations, Blankenship, now Triton's field manager, sank a six-inch drill down a test hole, called Borehole 10X, on higher and more stable ground some 180 feet northeast of the Pit during the summer of 1970. Before hitting bedrock at 180 feet, the drill went through several four-foot cavities and then entered a larger one at a depth of 230 feet. Several handfuls of a strange metal, somewhat similar in appearance to lead, were extracted from the drill hole. This material was analyzed by the Steel Company of Canada and found to be a form of smelted steel at least two hundred years old.

Encouraged by these discoveries, Triton had Borehole 10X widened to twenty-seven inches and lined to bedrock with one-quarter-inch steel casing the following winter. This was the twenty-ninth shaft sunk on the island and, like the others, it filled to sea level with water. During this operation, carried out mostly by Parker Kennedy, a Halifax-based professional driller, more of the soft metal was found. At 155 feet the drill came across a quantity of spruce and several small links of a steel chain analyzed to be at least two hundred years old. The fifty feet through the anhydrite bedrock to the seven-foot-high cavern remained unlined, but the twenty-seven-inch hole was large enough to allow a remote-controlled underwater camera to be lowered into the cavity in August 1971. This exciting enterprise, carried out with the assistance of the CBC in Halifax, produced some startling results. Blankenship, for whom the day is a memorable one, eagerly watched a monitor screen set up in a shed on the surface.

At first, as the camera was dropped into position, little could be seen except the wall of the narrow shaft. But then suddenly Blankenship was looking at what he believed was a severed human hand floating in the water. He called in others, including his assistant Dan Henskee, who still lives on the island, to take a look and they saw the same gruesome image. While the camera was being manoeuvred manually by ropes from the surface, the hand was apparently knocked to one side and disappeared. Later, to Blankenship's delight, the camera focused in on what looked like two or three chests. These large rectangular forms were covered with a layer of soft, whitish anhydrite and rested on the floor of the cavern. One had a distinctively curved top. What appeared to be the upright handle of a pickaxe or large hammer and several man-made timbers were closeby. A proturbance resembling the end of a squared timber stuck out below the roof of the cavity. Then the camera picked up what appeared to be details of a partly preserved human body lying slumped against the wall of the cavern. The water current in the cavern and the loose particles from the chalk-like bedrock made it difficult to hold the camera in place or to get greater detail. Blackenship took photographs of these remarkable images on the monitor, but the resulting prints are far from convincing.

According to project coordinator Kerry Allard of Montreal, the clearest of these photograpghs definitely showed a cavern approximately twelve feet by eighteen feet and about seven feet high. Ellard says the cavity appeared to have a tunnel leading off towards the direction of the shore, and the inrushing water seemed to confirm that a man-made or natural connection existed between the cavern and the sea. Referring to a photo of an upright piece of wood, he said, "We don't pretend to know exactly what the upright piece of wood is or whether it was put there by man. However, it seems clear from its position that it isn't natural."

When I first read about this dramatic event, one that seemed finally to prove that a treasure exists, and knowing that Triton had already invested hundreds of thousands of dollars in the venture, I naturally assumed that there was a tape or film of the sequence. During our first meeting, I questioned Blankenship about this and found it hard to believe what he told me, that no such record exists. Having worked in the news media for several years, I naturally felt

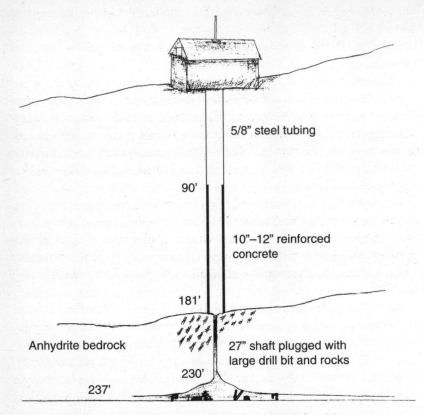

Bore Hole 10X: Chest-like shapes, timbers, tools and human remains were viewed by an underwater camera.

Triton was either working with extremely inexperienced people, was economizing severely or that a tape actually existed but was being withheld for some reason. The latter turned out to be the case.

Regardless of the skepticism of others at the time, Blankenship was convinced on that August afternoon in 1971 of the validity of what he saw on the monitor screen. His conviction, together with the evidence of man-made workings brought to light by earlier drilling in the area, led to the hiring of a professional diving company to explore the depths. After initial trouble from the pressure of the sea-water entering somewhere below the 180-foot level, possibly by way of a third flood tunnel, a diver succeeded in making his way down through the narrow shaft to the cavern at 230 feet. However, because the hole through the andhydrite bedrock had not been lined, the chalk-like material was disturbed by the diver's descent and it was impossible to see beyond a few inches in the milky waters. Eventually Blankenship himself descended into the cavern, but neither he nor other divers found anything during several courageous attempts.

The whole situation was extremely risky because of the pressure of the inflowing water, the continual pumping process and the solubility of the bedrock, so neither Blankenship nor the others actually ventured very far away from the narrow opening above their heads. It was later discovered that the pumping was severely eroding the bedrock within the cavern, which was eventually considered too dangerous to re-enter.

During 1973 and the following year, Blankenship sank several drill holes north of the treasure pit. One of these, some 660 feet to the northeast, was developed into a twelve by six foot shaft after a piece of wire and a metal plate were encountered below the 100-foot level, but the persistant inflow of fresh water led to its abandonment in 1974.

In 1976, after additional futile drillings in the Pit area, Blankenship turned his attention to Borehole 10X once again. Special sonar equipment developed by Bill Parkins, a weapons systems designer from Massachusetts and one of Triton's shareholders, produced readings which confirmed the presence of several other cavities above the bedrock. Blankenship was determined to explore Borehole 10X further, and a pump capable of moving 1,000 gallons per minute was put to work. Later, even more powerful pumps were put to work in an attempt to keep the water down close to bedrock level. Blankenship intended to cut through the metal casing at various levels to see if the cavities held anything of significance. He was ready to begin work in August 1976, but one of the powerful pumps ominously broke down, causing a delay. Finally in late September the work got under way, but the several holes cut into the metal casing yielded negative results.

Then, on a mid-November day, Dan Blankenship came within seconds of being buried alive in the bowels of the island when the walls of the narrow shaft began to crush inwards around the cable above his head as he hung strapped to a seat at the 140-foot level. After hearing a noise from within the shaft and being hit by bits of falling clay, he quickly realized the casing above his head was collapsing. He immediately yelled out for help on the telephone link to his son David, who was standing by at the winch-head above the opening of the shaft. David frantically hauled his father up in short order, but Dan reached the surface only seconds before the metal casing at the ninety-foot level crumpled inward like crushed cardboard as soil and rocks from the surrounding area began to pour in and completely block the shaft.

It was later ascertained that the continuous pumping had created an artificial fault close to the shaft, and that tons of soil and rocks had ultimately crashed against the casing with tremendous pressure, causing it to collapse.

In spite of this close brush with death, Dan remained determined to reach the treasure he was sure existed in the cavern at 230 feet, and so he developed a plan to make Borehole 10X completely secure. During 1978 he began to widen it and install eight-foot-wide solid steel cylinders welded together end to end to reinforce the unstable wall of the shaft. These were gradually sunk to the ninety-foot level, and the rest of the shaft to bedrock was afterwards lined with ten-inch-thick reinforced concrete. To Blankenship's obvious disappointment, the syndicate abandoned the project before it could be completed. The ever-persistant Oak Island jinx had struck again.

In the late 1970s Triton turned its attention once again to the treasure pit, with the intention of raising additional funds to finance a much deeper and wider shaft. However, before this ambitious plan got under way, the syndicate embarked on a challenge of a different kind. Around 1983 all exploration work on the island came to a virtual standstill for several years while Tobias and Blankenship became embroiled in a bitter court case over property rights with Fred Nolan.

David Tobias, President of Oak Island Exploration Company.

Frederick Nolan, long time Oak Island treasure searcher.

Dan Blankenship holding a leather shoe found nine feet under the beach and said to be hundreds of years old.

Parapsychologist Terry Murphy, one of several psychics who have provided insights into the Oak Island mystery.

The causeway leading from the mainland onto Oak Island at Crandall's Point.

Smith's Cove today. Site of the entrance to one of the underground flooding systems found on Oak Island.

Swamp area on Nolan's property in the center of the island where various discoveries have been made.

Site of Borehole 10X from Smith's cove where an underwater camera picked up images of timbers, tools and other objects in a cavern 230 feet below the surface.

The author pointing to the swamp from Nolan's latest excavation site.

One of the large, ten ton, granite boulders which form the cross found by Fred Nolan.

The G stone found by Dan Blankenship near the Cave-in pit.

Man drilled rock, one of several found on Oak Island.

Dagger or sword marking on the skull stone at the center of the cross.

Man made rock marker found on Oak Island by Fred Nolan.

```
         07·02·98
  12  2       16·95
Q         1
               1·19 IX
            18·14 M
         14·30
No  1       8193
```

12

The Oak Island Court Case

Many factors led to this lengthy and costly court case, which resolved the issue of land ownership on the island but has perpetuated ill will and mistrust between the opposing parties to this day.

The primary bases of the legal action were the imprecise and uncertain wording on the legal documents involved in the sale of the property from Lewis to Chappell many years earlier and Nolan's subsequently questionable acquisition of seven strategically placed lots in the centre of the island. Of course, other events had brought the friction between Triton Alliance and Nolan to a head.

In 1969, the year Tobias, Blankenship and others had formed Triton Alliance and attracted additional investors, there had been another breakdown in the agreement concerning the use of the causeway. Nolan had again blocked off access from the mainland at Crandall's Point, where he had constructed a small museum. Triton retaliated by building a small road around Nolan's property to the causeway, which Nolan was then prevented from using. He was forced once more to use a boat to get to his Oak Island lots at Joudrey's Cove. Determined to beat them at their own game, Nolan chained off the section of the island's one road which ran through his property. This meant Triton no longer had access on land to the treasure pit area and tempers flared.

One day Blankenship had approached Nolan with a rifle in hand and an ugly situation had begun to develop. Eventually the police were called in to calm everybody down and confiscate the gun. Triton had to spend additional time and money building its own road around Nolan's property along the edge of South Shore Cove. By November 1971 there was the first threat of a court case, but both sides were tired enough of the continuous jockeying for strategic position to be willing to negotiate a marriage of sorts. They compromised by giving each other access where needed and even agreed to exchange equipment and share information about their respective treasure searches.

For a few short years after 1971, the Nolan and Triton treasure hunts had proceeded with some degree of cooperation. Both parties had reason to believe they were on the right track. However, with the stakes high and bad blood already between them, it was a shaky relationship at best. The divorce became even more obviously inevitable when, in 1974, the Nova Scotia Department of Transportation widened the road at Crandall's Point to accommodate the increased summer tourist traffic to the island. Nolan objected, claiming the province had infringed on his property and promptly extended his museum building to block them off. The Department of Tourism quickly backed away from any future involvement, leaving the Oak Island cowboys to their own inevitable showdown. However, another fragile working agreement kept things moving forward for a few more years.

When Tobias bought Mel Chappell's one-hundred-acre holding on Oak Island in 1977 for $125,000, the Treasure Trove license, renewable every five years though the province's Department of Natural Resources, also changed hands. The arrangement with Nolan came unstuck once more, and from then on it was only a matter of time before the issue of property rights on the island came to a head. The antagonism went public in 1983 when Triton Alliance Ltd. launched a no-holds-barred lawsuit against Frederick Nolan, challenging his ownership of the seven centre island lots and claiming damages for loss of tourism business. The lawsuit not only brought the treasure hunt on Oak Island almost to a halt for several years but added substantially to its already high cost. During the hard-fought court case, Nolan admitted he had already spent in excess of $200,000 searching for the Oak Island treasure, and Triton stated it had invested over $1 million. It was estimated at the time that more than $2 million in total had been spent in attempts to solve the Oak Island mystery.

The case, heard by the Supreme Court of Nova Scotia in the nearby town of Bridgewater in May 1985, attracted much attention. The fact that it involved Oak Island was an attraction in itself, and by some it was seen as a David and Goliath struggle with the little guy, a local Nova Scotian, up against the financial might of a business syndicate whose well-heeled members were mostly "from away."

When the much-awaited decision by Justice A.M. MacIntosh was made public on January 1, 1986, Nolan was confirmed as the legal title holder of the disputed lots. But he was ordered not to interfere with access to the causeway, which the judge pointed out had been built across Crown land, and was ordered to compensate Triton to the tune of $15,000 for loss of tourism business.

Not content with the decision, and to many people's surprise, Triton appealed. In the April 1987 appeal court ruling the syndicate lost again. This time the compensation payment previously assessed against Nolan was reduced to $500 as the result of a counter appeal he had launched at the same time. Triton still had legal control of access to the island via the causeway, and so Nolan was forced to continue to use a boat from Crandall's Point to get to his property, a task he has carried out with dogged perseverance ever since.

Not much in the way of treasure hunting went on as both parties had prepared and presented their cases. Oak Island had succeeded in postponing the discovery of its elusive treasure for at least a few more years and was exacting an increasingly higher price. The court cases had cost both parties around $100,000 each, a sum Nolan could ill afford. Some of Triton's investors were not too pleased by the additional outlay and the extended delay. With the thorny matters of property rights and access settled, the bruised and battered parties were more anxious than ever to get back to work.

In a gesture of pragmatic acceptance, Tobias approached Nolan after the conclusion of the acrimonious legal action in 1987 with an outstretched hand and offered him a cigar. Nolan, who had been personally and professionally hurt by the case, responded cooly. Feelings of suspicion and mistrust ran too deep for a sudden heartfelt reconciliation between the two men. Besides, as he revealed to me one day on the porch of his cottage at Crandall's Point, Nolan had been quietly planning his own unique kind of retaliation, which was to involve his most dramatic discovery to date.

13

Deeper in the Hole

In July 1987, some months after the conclusion of the court case, and eighteen years and at least $1 million after their initial optimistic announcement back in 1969, the Triton directors went public with details of an astonishing but impressive plan which they claimed would finally solve the Oak Island mystery. Apart from the six lives lost and the devastation of much of the eastern end of the island, the financial cost of the treasure search had increased astronomically since that summer day in 1795 when Daniel McGinnis had taken a shovel to the circular depression in the ground. But the cost of Triton's ambitious plan was to drastically exceed even the $2 million estimated to have been incurred during the previous 190 years.

Triton announced with a good deal of publicity that, based on the best evidence available, all previous efforts and a consulting engineer's detailed report, a $1 million plan to recover the Oak Island treasure was about to be embarked upon. The large sum was needed to create the widest and deepest shaft ever dug on Oak Island. Encompassing all the shafts sunk earlier in the region of the treasure pit, this one was to be 80 feet wide and at least 215 feet deep. Underground mining specialists William Cox and Associates of Ottawa had been hired to design and construct the huge shaft, which David Tobias claimed should bring an end to the Oak Island mystery once and for all. In numerous interviews he exuded confidence in the plan and extolled the benefits of the project. For Tobias, it had become much more than a hunt for pirate's gold; it had evolved into something much more exciting and significant:

> This will be the largest undertaking of its kind on this side of the Atlantic. It is going to be a very professional, very methodical determination of what the island's ancient workings were built to protect. . . . This project is going to make history and it's going to be good for the people of Western Shore, the province of Nova Scotia and Canada as a whole. . . . Our artifacts and carbon dating results point

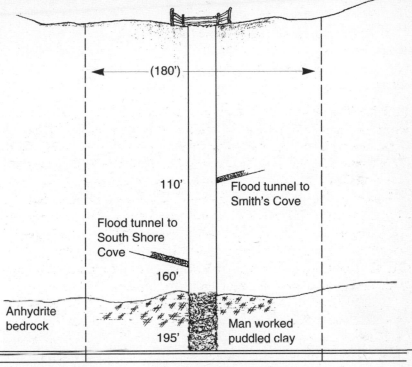

Triton's drilling discoveries in the Pit area and proposed large shaft.

original workings of the Pit as dating back to the sixteenth century. They would coincide with the second or third voyage of Francis Drake. . . . Even if there is no treasure, the findings will have historic and archaeological significance. . . . This is potentially a site with tremendous archaeological interest. This is important for Canada. . . . It's a national legacy.

With these and other equally impressive comments, Tobias launched the most ambitious and the most expensive Oak Island treasure hunt ever. In reports published widely in newspapers and magazines, he indicated the financing would be raised through public or private shares or through a limited partnership. A prospectus was sent out to underwriters in Canada and the U.S., and several securities companies expressed interest in negotiating a share offering of the company. Everything looked promising for a final assault on the Oak Island mystery.

Cox, the consulting engineer, was quoted as saying the huge shaft would be lined with a steel caisson to at least bedrock at 200 feet, and that any flood tunnels encountered on the way down would be blocked off with cement. Over one million cubic feet of earth was to be dug up, and several pumping stations, each capable of handling over a thousand gallons per minute, would keep the shaft completely dry. In addition, coffer dams would be constructed in Smith's Cove and South Shore Cove. Cox expressed confidence that the operation would expose whatever had been hidden in the depths of Oak Island, and that, once started, the actual shaft would be completed within six months. "It will be the decisive conclusion to Oak Island."

The provincial and national media gave extensive coverage to the story, and soon afterwards author D'Arcy O'Connor brought out an updated and timely version of his earlier book which he appropriately titled *The Big Dig*. Many people were flabbergasted by the scale and cost of the project, but most believed, on the basis of what was being proposed, that Triton would succeed where others had failed.

But this was not to be. Weeks passed into months and soon a year went by, but the necessary financing never materialized. Nobody had anticipated the long-term financial consequences of Black Monday, the day in October 1987 when the stock markets took a severe nose dive. For a long time afterwards, investors were extremely shy of new and untried stock, especially when it might involve a venture as risky as a search for buried treasure. In some financial circles the Oak Island project became the joke of the month. By April 1988, Tobias and the other directors of Triton had realized that their dream of raising $10 million on the North American markets was not going to be fulfilled. Tobias's understatement at the time was: "Market trends were not in our favour."

However, Triton was not about to throw in the towel. Alternative approaches to raise the necessary funds were in the works. One involved trying to presell live television rights to the dig, as had been done with other projects, the most well-known example being the much-publicized opening of Al Capone's personal safe.

In December 1989 Triton acquired control of a New York trading company, Northeast Capital Inc., and changed its name to Oak Island Exploration Company. By January 1990 the fifty shareholders had a public investment vehicle by which they could proceed to sell newly issued shares offshore.

The *Financial Post* of February 5, 1990, quoted Norman Tobias, David's son and a director of the newly formed company, as saying he anticipated no difficulty in registering the newly issued shares once they had been disposed of. About the same time, Triton's entire Oak Island property, with the exception of two lots, was reregistered in the name of Oak Island Tours Inc. Blankenship retained owner-ship of Lot 23, a four-acre holding just east of the causeway on which he had built his house in 1975. Lot 25, a little further to the southeast, remained in Tobias's name.

During 1991 the company approached the provincial and federal governments in the hope of either getting a $12-million loan guaran-tee or tax incentives for potential investors. It was turned down on both counts. Officials at the Atlantic Canada Opportunities Agency (ACOA) found it hard to embrace such a mercurial proposal; the Nova Scotia Department of Tourism declined financial help, even though Tobias argued that the project would create fifty jobs and promote tourism in a depressed area; and federal Minister of Finance Don Mazankowski rejected the application for tax concessions. Tobias was bitterly disappointed because he had been hoping a show of government support would kickstart his company's stalled plans.

Failure to raise the necessary capital meant the Oak Island Exploration Company, which had taken over the license and media rights to the project, had to hold off its plans for the massive excava-tion project or risk a less costly approach to getting at the treasure. This was the same old dilemma that had plagued many previous treasure searches on Oak Island. Too many frustrating failures had already resulted from lack of sufficient financing and the necessary equipment for Tobias and company to be keen to embark on a risky course that could result in yet another. So, during much of 1992, while the syndicate's directors considered their options, the Oak Island Exploration Company carried out relatively little exploration work on the island and hardly any information was given out to a now constantly curious media. The welcome mat had been laid out for writers and reporters not long before my arrival on the scene, but the now evasive Blankenship told me in our first phone conversation later that year that he "didn't see a need to keep the media or the public abreast of what is going on." It was obvious to anyone visit-ing the east end of the island that summer that not much was.

14

The Search Continues

Within a few weeks of beginning my research into the Oak Island mystery, I came across information concerning Nolan's discovery of the large stone cross. A brief article in the Halifax *Chronicle-Herald*, written by reporter Steve Proctor, quoted the normally tight-lipped surveyor as saying that sometime in the past people with advanced knowledge had been at work on the island. I phoned Nolan and in answer to my initial question he adamantly asserted that the cross was not a natural phenomenon created by glacial action but had been constructed by human effort, a conclusion later confirmed by Halifax geologist Petra Mudie. After asking Nolan several questions about the precise details of the structure's discovery, layout and appearance, he agreed to meet with me and discuss the matter further.

During a lengthy discussion at his Crandall's Point cottage on a mild January day in 1993, he calmly explained to me how he had gradually uncovered the structure during the early 1980s while shooting transit lines across his property and after cleaning out over-grown areas. He had spent several years carefully excavating around and beneath some of the boulders after methodically marking out their positions, measurements and orientations. He described how he and a co-worker found a layer of small beach stones and parts of a ship's pot-belly stove under the boulder at the end of the south arm of the cross. He could not explain how either happened to be there. Convinced in his own mind that the structure was man-made, Nolan had it examined and verified by Halifax-based engineer and survey-or William Crooker before going public with the details in the summer of 1992. In answer to my final question that day, Nolan insisted that no boulders of similiar size or shape existed elsewhere in the vicinity.

Several months later I was able to see the proof of Nolan's claim for myself. I got to view the cross while touring the treasure pit site alongside a British television crew, who were filming for a series on treasure islands in April 1993. I found it as Nolan said I would, with the large boulders perfectly in line and precisely positioned. As I walked around the extensive site in the centre of Nolan's property, it occurred to me that, in spite of the precision involved, nature might still have been responsible for the unusual positions of the boulders. I later discussed the matter with a geologist at the Nova Scotia Museum of Natural History, who, admitting he had not carried out a detailed study of the structure or the surrounding area, was of the opinion that the boulders had most probably been deposited by glaciers. However, the conclusion of geologist Petra Mudie after two close examinations of the site was entirely the opposite.

What made my first visit to Nolan's part of the island even more interesting was that, as I wandered around his property, which is not accessible to the public, I suddenly saw the exact location shown to me months before by the young girl in my dream. I mentioned this to Nolan during one of our meetings in the summer of 1993 and his reaction indicated to me that he had his own good reasons for believing the site was of significance. When I later asked him if he was digging in that area, he refused to discuss the matter further, but more than a year later I discovered he had in fact been exploring there.

During one of my many conversations with Nolan, he confided that it was the dramatic discovery of the cross and its implications he had had in mind when he had exchanged cool formalities with Tobias after the conclusion of the court appeal in 1987. The publicity concerning the cross came at a time when the Triton operation was almost at a standstill and drew attention to the Nolan treasure hunt in particular. Although Nolan was reticent to discuss other, possibly symbolic, implications of the cross, the announcement of its discovery had also refocused interest on theories which indicated the mystery and the treasure itself might have a religious connection.

Prior to the October 1993 Oak Island Conference I helped to organize, Nolan informed a mutual friend, Charles Crowell, that he had been excavating a new site northeast of the head of the cross. Without supplying precise details, he explained he had been led to the site by a series of calculations involving "significant rocks." He claimed he had removed the surface soil and found a distinctively square-shaped grouping of large granite boulders and the top centre stone had a cross carved into it. Nolan had quickly removed the boulders and dug down some twenty feet in the hope of discovering an underground vault, but there was no opening and no treasure. I visited the site with others attending the conference, but all we found was a large empty crater and a scattered pile of nondescript rocks nearby. Attempts to locate the inscribed centre stone were unsuccessful. When I later remarked that from a researcher's standpoint he had perhaps been a little too hasty and careless in dismantling the alleged structure, the self-reliant and independent-minded Nolan seemed annoyed.

During the summer of 1994, Nolan returned to excavating in an area on the west side of the swamp. He cut down some trees and began to dig near a location where he had previously found what he claimed was a small stone monument. This was about 150 feet southeast of the bottom boulder of the cross; it was also not far from the location indicated in my first dream about Oak Island. By late fall he had finished excavation work for the year, and during my visit to the island with Dr. Mudie and others in December 1994, we noticed that an area had been refilled. Perhaps he has found something of note in the location and will continue to work this site in the future. Undoubtedly he will keep any discovery a secret until he is ready to reveal his findings.

Earlier that same summer, Nolan told me he intended to reopen his small museum at Crandall's Point. He showed me a large detailed map highlighting his own discoveries which he had produced for the occasion. The map indicated that a treasure site lay just northeast of the head of the cross, the site where Nolan had uncovered the large stone construction. The sparse and badly neglected museum, which, like its counterpart on the other side of the causeway, needed renovating and upgrading, closed after a few weeks due to lack of interest.

In my several meetings with Nolan between 1993 and 1995, he never wavered from his deeply held conviction that an undertaking of incredible proportions took place on Oak Island hundreds of years ago and that it involved individuals with a knowledge of engineering, mathematics and symbolism. Very much the loner, Nolan has apparently shouldered the enormous cost of trying to get to the bottom of the Oak Island mystery almost entirely by himself. Yet for him, and Dan Blankenship, the cost has been much more than financial. A good deal of both their lives for the past thirty years has been consumed by an unrelenting desire to be the first to find the treasure and by the many demands and challenges involved in their different approaches. The rivalry, competition, underlying friction and open conflict has also taken its toll. The strain is clearly apparent at times on their faces and in their-less guarded comments. The high personal price can only be known by those who have themselves fallen victim to the treasure-hunting spell.

"No one would believe me if I told them what I thought, so I'll continue to work away until I find the treasure or die in the process. I've put so much into this and seen so much that I can't turn back now. I guess in a way I've created my own living hell and it's not easy to get out of it." With these stark words, spoken during our meeting in December 1994, Nolan candidly acknowledged the predicament he finds himself in. Strangely enough, much the same sentiment had been expressed by Blankenship several years earlier. In an interview with a British newspaper, he answered a question about how long he intended to pursue the search with a chilling, curt comment: "I'm here now until I get the treasure or it gets me." These were not idle words, because not long before Blankenship had come within seconds of being the seventh man to lose his life while risking all to find the Oak Island treasure.

Face to face for the first time with the still robust seventy-year-old Blankenship as we drove to the east end of the island on a cold April morning in 1993, I found him rigidly tight-lipped about his current activities on the island. But when I brought up Borehole 10X, his attitude changed remarkably. As the car rattled along the narrow, winding road to the site of the Pit, he readily recalled some of the most exciting, dangerous and rewarding moments of his life on Oak Island. It was clear that the thrill of the search, the anticipation of the hunter and the determination of a man desperate to overcome adverse odds were in his blood. The conversation left no doubt in my mind that he was entirely convinced of the validity of the images he had seen on the monitor that day in August 1971. When I asked him if he would risk another descent into the cavern at the bottom of Borehole 10X, he did not hesitate to answer yes.

Later that same morning I peered down into the dark depths of the circular shaft, the mouth of which is enclosed in a metal shed, in the presence of a British television crew and heard one of them remark it was like looking into a hole into hell. In the ensuing silence, I thought about the hell Blankenship must have experienced during those terrible seconds when he had come close to being buried alive more than ninety feet below. One had to admire his courage.

Apart from rusting machinery and a long-abandoned shaft, there was little else to see in the area of the treasure pit. However, a short visit to the small and unfortunately neglected museum proved much more interesting. A congested assortment of items was on display in counter-top glass cases and on the walls. Included were samples of coconut fibre, wood and metal found deep underground and at Smith's Cove, and old graphs and charts ranging back to much earlier treasure hunts. I found a replica of the hieroglyphically inscribed stone found ninety feet down in the Pit of particular interest but was most compelled by the several blurred photographs of images Blankenship claims to have seen on the monitor in 1971.

During the following two summers, I revisited the museum and, with Dan and Fred's permission, the various sites several times. Nolan eventually showed me some of the items he had found on the island over the years, and I talked with both men about various aspects of the treasure search as the occasion prompted and time and temperaments allowed.

In mid-October 1993, while preparing material for the Oak Island Conference, I learned there had indeed been a videotape recording of the interior of the cavern at the bottom of Borehole 10X. After finishing a live television interview with Blankenship at the site of the treasure pit on the day of the conference, I confronted him with this information and he admitted that what I had suspected all along was true.

Apparently the tape had been of poor quality and the images unconvincing. It had been put aside and had laid on a shelf for more than twenty years. I later learned that when new investor Bob Atkinson had arrived on the scene late in 1993, Blankenship had resurrected the long forgotten videotape. Following their discussions with Bob Frank, the amiable economic development officer for Lunenburg County, with a view to reactivating interest in the project, the old one-inch tape was re-examined and it was decided to have it computer cleaned and enhanced. As a result of this process, carried out by a U.S. company, some of the images seen by Blankenship on the monitor over twenty years earlier had become much clearer and more defined. During the course of a lengthy conversation I had with Frank at his Bridgewater office in early January 1995, he described having seen stills taken from the cleaned tape which showed two chests resting on the floor of the cavern. According to Frank, Atkinson had also financed an extensive sonic and water testing program in the area around the Pit. This series of tests, reputed to have cost between $200,000 and $300,000, had apparently not resulted in much new information. However, what was learned may help confirm the best location for any new attempts to reach openings below bedrock.

In a telephone conversation with David Tobias in Montreal a few days later, Tobias told me that photographs from the tape would be released "at an appropriate time," possibly through the channels of a public relations agency or as part of a media package. In several subsequent telephone conversations, he repeatedly turned down my requests to include the photos in this book, but he indicated that decisions being considered at a weekend board meeting at the Oak Island Inn in mid-January 1995 might result in some "new developments" in this regard.

Then, in what may have been an independent action on his part, Blankenship, who has not always agreed with plans devised by Tobias or other members of the syndicate, and who for years has refused to speak in public, set up an unprecedented public meeting at the Western Shore firehall on Sunday, March 5, 1995. At the well-attended event, he produced a thirty-minute extract and a series of still photographs from the underground film shot with the help of the CBC back in 1971. It was evident that Blankenship was pleased to be able to demonstrate that his long pursuit of the Oak Island treasure had not been entirely in vain and that his convictions about the merits of Borehole 10X had substance.

The computer cleaned and enhanced tape clearly showed the interior of Borehole 10X as the camera descended into the water-filled cavern some 230 feet below the surface. Within the cavern was strong visual evidence of entrances to two tunnels. Several camera angles provided different views of possible wooden cribbing and what seemed like an upright wooden post. There was a clear picture of the handle of either a pick or a sledge hammer standing upright on the ground. The camera had also focused on what could be two wooden chests buried under a blanket of anhydrite sediment. The tape also showed images of what Blankenship claimed was a human head and hand.

As the images passed before me, I readily accepted the fact that men had worked at this depth and that the cavern was another part of the extensive maze of underground workings created hundreds of years ago on Oak Island. Naturally I found myself wondering whether the dead person might be one of the original workers. I also wondered if the two wooden chests, believed to have disappeared after the collapse in the Pit nearly 150 years earlier had somehow fallen to this deeper level some two hundred feet away. The tape and photographs made interesting viewing and stimulated a good deal of discussion, but not eveyone who attended the event was convinced of Blankenship's suggestions and interpretations regarding the images.

Since being forced to abandon the shaft some years ago, Blankenship has always admitted he would like to have another chance to explore the cavern and retrieve whatever it contains. More recently, however, another diver experienced extreme difficulties during a descent and, after being hauled to the surface, was found to be suffering from a severe case of the "bends." Fortunately he recovered, but his diving days are over. To complicate matters, the existing entrance to the cavern through the bedrock at the bottom of Borehole 10X remains blocked off by rock and an embedded drill head, and the cavern remains extremely difficult and dangerous to enter.

To overcome these obstacles and guarantee greater safety, the twenty-year-old shaft casing to bedrock level needs to be extended downwards into the cavern itself, or a new shaft needs to be sunk elsewhere in the vicinity. With seawater coming in under enormous pressure, pumps capable of extracting a thousand gallons per minute would be required. The estimated cost is about about $350,000.

One of the politicians invited to the March 5th meeting was area MLA and Nova Scotia Fisheries Minister Jim Barkhouse who, after viewing the images, expressed his opinion that it was time government got involved. In a conversation with him a few days after the meeting, he suggested that although it was possible the province might fund a modern interpretation centre on the island as part of a tourist development project, it was unlikely that public funds would be forthcoming for exploration work.

Knowing that he may have only one last chance to get his hands on the treasure, Blankenship has been hoping for additional financial support. The tourism potential of Oak Island, something Blankenship has had little time for in the past, could be quite lucrative and is what the government is most interested in. It was not surprising that in early 1995 Blankenship showed up at a meeting of the South Shore Tourism Association and talked enthusiastically about the island's attraction as a tourist site, especially during a year which marks the two-hundreth anniversary of the discovery of the treasure pit.

While the Oak Island Exploration Company has been pursuing political and financial support, Blankenship has also been busy keeping other potential treasure hunters at bay. Small-scale excavations have already been initiated by at least three others on sites not far from Oak Island, and others were likely to follow as a result of the renewed publicity generated by the disclosure of the tape. First off the mark, Blankenship has acquired Treasure Trove licenses for twelve other islands and for three shoreline sites nearby. Encompassing seventy-two claims and 2,880 acres in total, the licenses are all issued in his name.

With the help of regional officials and local political insiders, who see an obvious potential for economic spinoffs from tourism, renewed exploration activity and greater publicity about the island, meetings have already been held with local politicians, the heads of government funding agencies and provincial Natural Resources Minister Don Downe. In a faxed response dated March 16, 1995, to questions I had earlier asked him, Downe emphasized the island's potential as a major tourist attraction. The Oak Island Exploration Company could probably end up getting some form of government support in exchange for allowing greater development of the island's tourism potential.

Armed with newly acquired scientific data, new radiocarbon C-14 test results and its recently acquired computer-enhanced images, the syndicate should also be able to raise the necessary funding for another attempt to explore the depths of Oak Island. According to Tobias, the number of shareholders in the company has increased dramatically from Triton's original fifty as of mid-February 1995. A new dig was likely to commence in the same year.

In view of the many past failures to retrieve the treasure by merely sinking deeper and larger holes, one should not discount the possibility that even if the treasure or part of it is in the cavern at the bottom of Borehole 10X, it may yet elude another attempt to bring it to the surface. Over the past two hundred years, Oak Island has repeatedly shown that it is capable of frustrating the best efforts of experienced engineers who have adopted this straightforward approach to get at the treasure. It seems an untried avenue may be necessary to finally solve the mystery.

Perhaps excavations on another part of the island, possibly adjacent to the swamp on adjoining property, would result in easier access to the underground workings. Nolan certainly thinks so. Were he and the principals of the Oak Island Exploration Company to put their differences behind them and work together, it could lead to a new era of cooperative and harmonious work on the island. The pooling of over sixty years of combined research and effort could result in a dramatic breakthrough. David Tobias expressed interest in this approach not too long ago and has contacted Nolan on several occasions. Of course, animosity, mistrust and desires to capitalize on their own investments may prove to be unsurmountable obstacles for the parties presently involved in the treasure hunt, and others may need to take up the challenge before Oak Island will reveal its most closely guarded secret.

The Oak Island phenomenon has by now achieved an international stature and has gained a place beside other great mysteries worldwide. It can even be argued that the physical treasure itself is by right a national legacy and the site too important archaeologically and historically for any one individual or party to have under their private control. Many people believe the buried treasure is far more important than the personal ambitions, pride or greed of any single treasure hunter and that the sharing of all pertinent information among genuine and proven researchers is long overdue in the interests of finally retrieving it. Laverne Johnson, who has openly disclosed the details behind his theory concerning the possible location of the treasure, called for much the same approach several years ago when he wrote: "If enough people could have the opportunity of learning what the evidence really indicates at Oak Island, it could change the whole direction of the search for the solution of the mystery."

As a consequence of acquiring his own treasure trove licences in July of 1994 Blankenship was obliged to resign from the board of the Oak Island Exploration Company. His action also raised some doubt about his future status as the company's field manager on the island. In addition his preoccupation with borehole 10X, which according to company president David Tobias is almost fanatical, resulted in additional differences between the two longtime partners.

Early in 1995 a completely new phase in the extensive and costly search for the treasure began with the arrival on the scene of Oak Island Discoveries Incorporated. This Boston based company headed by Don Glazer is reputed to have substantial financial backing. It has been hinted that the company is interested in producing a documentary film about Oak Island for worldwide distribution.

Perhaps more important is the fact that Oak Island Discoveries has entered into an agreement with the prestigious Woods Hole Institute of Massachusetts to carry out research both on and off the island. Personnel and equipment from Woods Hole under the direction of the flamboyant Bob Ballard participated in the successful attempt to locate the sunken wreck of the Titanic. According to institute director David Gallo all scientific activity will be carried out under the auspices of Oak Island Discoveries.

Following a flying visit to the island earlier this year by individuals from both organizations samples of wood and other materials were taken away for more sophisticated radiocarbon dating. Hopefully these latest tests will put to rest any uncertainty about the timeframe of the original work on the island. It is expected that a team of coastal technicians will carry out geological research in the waters around Oak Island later this summer. The institute's expertise may also be used on the island itself perhaps in an attempt to access and recover any items at the bottom of borehole 10X. This is an exciting development and one that may well prove successful where others have failed.

Meanwhile the island's other treasure hunter Fred Nolan is excited about two new discoveries on his property. One seems to be symbolic in nature and involves the carved out shape of a sword or dagger on the skull stone at the centre of the cross. The other is more substantial according to Nolan and has led him to undertake exploratory drilling at a site west of the swamp. In his final discussion with me earlier this summer he sounded as optimistic and enthusiastic as if he was just embarking on the treasure search for the first time.

Another interesting development occurred unexpectedly just prior to finishing this book. Following a lecture about Oak Island which I gave at the Chester theatre in June I was approached by parapsychologist Terry Murphy with new information she had received psychically about the historical background to the mystery and some of the prominent people involved.

There is no doubt that the search for the Oak Island treasure is as active and interesting as ever on this the two hundredth anniversary of its beginning.

15

Theories Ahoy!

While researching the Oak Island story, I was amazed and at times amused by the wide variety of theories concerning the origin and nature of the mysterious treasure. There seems to be a theory to fit just about every historical time-frame, from the prehistoric era and the legendary civilization of Atlantis to the days of the French Revolution of 1789. One theory even connects extraterrestials with the mystery.

In between the antediluvian Atlanteans and the interplanetary travellers are an eclectic assortment of middle-eastern and western cultures who, according to the proponents of the various theories, could have used Oak Island at one time or another. These include the ancient Egyptians and Greeks, Christian Arabs and Irish Celts. The Scots are represented, as are the English, French and Spanish. Peoples of more northern and southern climates are also credited with visiting Oak Island in theories that involve the Vikings and Incas. Of course, several privateers and pirates also figure prominently on the long and colourful list. Closer to home, the Acadians and the indigenous Mi'kmaq have also been believed to be behind the Oak Island enigma. The treasure itself is believed to include everything from Atlantean artifacts to war chests from the time of the revolt of the American colonies.

The first treasures hunters—McGinnis, Vaughan and Smith—were sure they would find a hoard of pirate's treasure, possibly that of Captain Kidd, just a few feet below the ground. After the discovery of the extensive underground workings, others came to believe that a large quantity of gold and jewels from the Spanish conquest of South America had been buried on the island, if not by the Spanish themselves, then by the likes of English privateer Sir Francis Drake. After the extensive water traps had been uncovered, still others concluded that there must have been a military involvement and that the treasure could be money in pay-chests concealed by the French or English during their seesawing struggle over Nova Scotia. Alternatively, it could be large quantities of valuables taken by

British forces from Havana in 1762, or from New York following the American Declaration of Independence in 1776. For a time, a few people even believed that part of the crown jewels of France had been shipped to Oak Island by troops loyal to the monarchy during the French Revolution.

Some people suggested that Oak Island was the hiding place of English and Scottish church treasures which went missing in the seventeenth century. The missing Inca wealth from the city of Tumbez in Peru was a favoured theory of others. Some suggested that the Knights Templar had brought the Holy Grail or other early Christian relics across the Atlantic to Oak Island. The discovery of the piece of parchment, one of the few pieces of tangible evidence that something of possible intellectual or literary interest was buried on the island, gave rise to speculation that the treasure could contain the missing original Shakespearean manuscripts credited to Sir Francis Bacon.

The unique geological nature of Oak Island has encouraged a wide range of theories concerning the origin of the mystery. Belonging to a rock formation known as the Windsor group, which is dominant elsewhere in Nova Scotia, the island is part of a small geological anomaly on the province's south shore. The fact that naturally formed underground caverns are present in the island's bedrock has led some Oak Island speculators to wonder whether an ancient civilization might have used the location to store its records or valuables. Some have even suggested that perhaps Oak Island has been used on more than one occasion to bury things of value, and that these workings and deposits may have occurred hundreds or even thousands of years apart.

The theory that Atlanteans had used Oak Island was interesting to me, if for no other reason than that I had previously done some research and written about the famous fabled lost continent after a marble pillar, a strange monolith and a megalithic roadway were discovered underwater off the island of Bimini in the Bahamas. Sources such as the Greek philosopher Plato and Celtic mythology suggest the civilization existed at one time in the mid-Atlantic, information the psychic Edgar Cayce elaborated on in some detail.

From what I learned from the writings of Ignatius Donnelly, the Cayce material and articles published by explorer David Zinck and others about the fabled advanced civilization, said to have self-destructed some 12,000 years ago, the Atlanteans possessed extraordinary abilities and probably would have constructed something much more sophisticated than what has been discovered on the island, assuming it even existed as an island at that time. Anyway, the theory that Atlanteans were involved falls completely apart when one considers the dates established by the radiocarbon dating of wood samples taken from the man-made workings found on the island. However, a connection may exist in the fact that the legendary Atlantis was an inspiration behind some of Sir Francis Bacon's philosophical writings, which in turn influenced seventeenth-century Masonic and Rosicrucian thinking.

The question of whether the native people of Nova Scotia, the Mi'kmaq, are responsible for the Oak Island mystery has been raised repeatedly and I also felt obliged to explore this possibility. The Mi'kmaq, like the Maliseet and the Beothuk, lived along the northeastern seaboard of the North American continent for thousands of years prior to the arrival of Norse adventurers, Basque fishermen, and Scottish, French and English explorers. They lived a nomadic life, setting up camps along riverbanks and ocean shorelines in the summer when fish were plentiful, and moving inland in the winter for shelter and for game that provided meat and clothing. No evidence of a Mi'kmaq campsite has been found close to Oak Island, nor did they possess the tools necessary for such an extensive undertaking. I was naturally curious about their legends, hoping in them to find a clue to the origin of the mystery. However, apart from the stories of the divine figure Kluscap (Glooscap), I could find nothing remotely associating the Mi'kmaq of the past with Oak Island.

Much the same can be said of the first Europeans known to have visited this part of the world. More than a thousand years ago, seagoing Norsemen from Scandinavia crossed the hazardous northern Atlantic as far as Iceland and Greenland where they set up small settlements. Then, led by the stalwart Leif Ericsson, a group of these Vikings reached North America, landing first on Baffin Island and the coast of Labrador. These journeys and their travels further south became part of the Norse Sagas, the possible authenticity of which, like the legends of Troy and Atlantis, was ignored or discounted for centuries by archaeologists and historians. Fortunately, mostly due to the determination of a Norwegian writer, the Norse settlement at L'Anse aux Meadows on the northern tip of Newfoundland was unearthed in 1961. However, it is unlikely that the Norse of that era were capable of carrying out the work found on Oak Island, and the time-frame established by radiocarbon dating contradicts any such connection.

A theory I found interesting because of its possible Knights Templar and Masonic connections was one involving the much-disputed voyage of the fourteenth-century Earl of Orkney, Prince Henry St. Clair. The 1398 voyage was described in detail in a document known as the "Zeno Narrative" by Venetian navigator Antonio Zen. Historian and author Frederick Pohl has documented landfall descriptions in the narrative which match coastal locations in Nova Scotia. Ever since, there has been speculation that St. Clair, whose family had been involved in the Crusades to Jerusalem and had given safe refuge to Templars after their excommunication by Pope Clement V in 1307, may have brought some of the reputed missing Templar treasures, including sacred relics, to the New World.

The claim made a few years ago by a former resident of New Ross, located at the headwaters of the Gold River not far from Oak Island, that a low wall unearthed on her property was actually part of the foundation of a castle used by St. Clair and others served to fuel speculation connecting the Knights Templar and their sacred treasure to Oak Island.

Already, the Nova Scotia communities of Guysborough and St. Peter's, where St. Clair is believed to have landed, plan to recognize the legitimacy of the voyage. If the voyage did take place—and based on accepted fourteenth-century navigational history it is certainly a possibility—then St. Clair and his men could have been responsible for some activity on Oak Island prior to that established by radiocarbon dating.

The men who first discovered the treasure pit in 1795 believed they had found the hiding place of pirates' loot. This was the natural and easiest assumption to make, and there are several likely candidates, with the New York–based Captain Kidd topping the list.

Stories both real and imagined of Kidd's exploits on the high seas, his execution in London in 1701 and his reputed buried treasure have become part of maritime lore along the eastern seaboard. However, as the nature and magnitude of the underground workings became more apparent in 1850, it was clear that a large body of skilled men must have been involved. Some treasure hunters at the time concluded that Oak Island must have been used as a pirates' communal bank and involved others beside Captain Kidd.

Most researchers, myself included, quickly dismiss the pirate theory, not only because of the extensiveness of the original workings, which would have required knowledge of mining and marine engineering, but also because the project obviously required a small army of experienced and disciplined men working cooperatively under an effective authority structure. And secrecy was an essential component in the planning and execution of the project. When all these factors are considered, the theory that Oak Island was used by roaming pirates as a place to stash their collective booty just does not hold up. Pillage, plunder and pleasure were the pursuits of most pirates, who were not known for their mutual trust or interest in long-term security. Some theorists who favour a pirate involvement in Oak Island point to the seventeenth-century stronghold of Port Royal on the coast of Jamaica as an example of pirate ingenuity and cooperativeness. But no communal bank ever existed in that pirates' den, which was destroyed by an earthquake in 1692. Most pirates died while engaged in their reckless and notorious trade, hung, as it were, by their own petard, their treasure spent or hidden somewhere known only to themselves.

However, researching the lives and times of such individuals, one soon learns that just as there were many purely self-serving, lawless pirates such as Peter Easton, Edward Teach and David Bassett, there were also licensed privateers. These freelancing, adventurous and militant seafarers such as Sir Francis Drake and Sir William Phipps were for the most part law-abiding, at least as far as serving the interests of their own countries was concerned. Sometimes, as in the case of Captain William Kidd, Captain Henry Morgan and others, they turned out to be both pirate and privateer.

It occurred to me as I investigated their activities that there was a remote possibility that one of these maritime mercenaries could have been secretly hired by other parties to find a suitable hiding place for a valuable treasure. Because the rulers of sixteenth- and seventeenth-century England and France licensed privateers to attack and raid each other's ships and settlements in the New World, because English privateers were attacking and looting Spanish ships in the Caribbean and because trading companies hired privateers to protect their interests on the high seas, such a scenario is not implausible. It could also account for the original and persistent association between so-called "pirates" and Oak Island.

It has been estimated that the man-made constructions found to date on Oak Island would have required an army of men working in a disciplined fashion for as long as two years. This has led to theories that the French or British militaries, with their authority structures, engineering expertise, manpower and abilities to maintain secrecy, must have been involved.

During the nearly 150 years from the establishment of their first small trading enterprise in the New World to the surrender of their extensive North American colonies to England in 1763, the French had on different occasions sent out shiploads of soldiers and settlers, professionals and tradesmen, and money and supplies to their New France. There had in fact been a French settlement not far from Oak Island at LaHave in the early seventeenth century that had military personnel among its members. This has led to the theory that the French used Oak Island as a temporary bank on at least one occasion, perhaps during the conflict with the British at Louisbourg. The same theory under a different flag had the English temporarily storing the contents of a pay ship on Oak Island. As mentioned, it has also been suggested that senior British naval officers used the island to hide riches taken from Havana after it was seized from the Spanish in 1762. Given the many skilled and disciplined men at their disposal, either power would certainly have been capable of constructing the workings found on the island.

Another theory with a military flavour relates to the American War of Independence. Following the famous Boston Tea Party and the outbreak of hostilities at Concord and Lexington in 1775, the British suffered some very humiliating and worrisome defeats. General William Howe chose to retreat with the Nova Scotia garrison and fleet from Boston to Halifax after being besieged by Washington's forces. Another debacle early in the campaign to stamp out the upstart colonists was the surrender of a large force under General Sir John Burgoyne at Saratoga in 1777. Some have suggested that in the years leading up to and immediately following the decisive defeat at Yorktown in 1782 the British command under Jeffrey Amherst, William Howe, Henry Clinton or Charles Cornwallis may have removed important colonial documents and other valuables from the thirteen colonies and deposited them in a underground vault on Oak Island.

The widespread presence of Masonic lodges and Masonic thinking among the highest levels of the French and English military command going back hundreds of years allows one to make a strong case for the involvement of senior military personnel in a secret civilian mission involving the elaborate concealment and protection of a Fraternity-related treasure on Oak Island.

My research into the significance of many of the symbols and rock structures found on Oak Island has led me to the conclusion that there is a Masonic or Rosicrucian connection to the mystery. Radiocarbon and other dating methods applied to samples of various materials found on the island have established a 150-year window from 1500 to 1650 as the most likely time the elaborate underground work was carried out. In trying to determine which historical group or figure of that period would have had the appropriate motive and been capable of instigating such an intricate project, I have concluded that the person in question was most likely the brilliant Elizabethan Sir Francis Bacon, whose associates, Masonic and otherwise, had knowledge of and access to Nova Scotia.

16

An Elizabethan Adventure

Could one or more of the Elizabethan English explorers have visited Oak Island in their many trips to the New World while involved in a conspiracy—one of the many at the time—and concealed some treasure there? A brief examination of historical facts supports this possibility.

Towards the end of the long and resplendent reign of its unquestionably vigorous but doubtfully virginal Queen Elizabeth I, England began to view itself as a potential world power. The British had proved their superiority at sea, and in the words of the philosophically minded man of action Sir Walter Raleigh, who knew only too well about such things, "whoever rules the sea commands the trade; whoever commands the trade commands the riches of the world and consequently even the world itself."

With the turgid and much troubled Henry VIII as her father, Elizabeth's childhood, upbringing, education and unexpected ascent to the throne of England was a wild adventure and a story of personal survival. Having lost her mother to the executioner's axe, she was disowned by her father, banished from the court, ostracised by the aristocracy as an illegitimate offspring and later interred in the Tower of London for treason. It is not surprising that this abandoned and love-deprived, frightened but highly intelligent young woman sought solace in the arms of fellow prisoner Robert Dudley, Earl of Leicester. It has long been argued that she and Dudley were secretly married in prison, a marriage that was later annulled. The *Dictionary of National Biography* mentions the relationship and the rumours, circulating even during Elizabeth's reign, that she and Dudley had had a son. Many researchers into this aspect of Elizabeth's life have concluded that the love child was none other than Sir Francis Bacon, who was secretly adopted and reared by sympathetic friends Sir Nicholas and Lady Bacon in order to protect Elizabeth's reputation and hold on the throne. Molded by her extraordinary past, she was able to maintain her reign, bring a good measure of stability to her country's affairs and increase England's power and wealth with the help of some exceptionally gifted men.

Thanks to the superior seamanship of Francis Drake, John Hawkins and Thomas Howard, the once dominant Spanish, with their self-righteous religious airs, their enormous new-found wealth from the Americas and their threatening armadas, had been put in their place. But although the Spanish King Philip II continued to strut his stuff on the high seas, the otherwise bold young queen of England was hesitant to openly commit her country to transatlantic adventures and colonial expansion. Despite the urgings of her geographer and nautical expert, the quixotic John Dee, she was content to let the likes of the daredevil Drake risk reputations and lives on her behalf.

Dee, whose later associates included the philosophically minded Sir Francis Bacon and Robert Fludd, both of whom worked on the King James translation of the Bible, was also an avid astrologer, mathematician and mystic. He was a leading member of the "Rosicrucian Enlightenment," an esoteric Christian-based spiritual movement that attracted many philosophers, artists, scientists and writers in England and Europe, especially Germany, where John Andrea Valentine published the first known works on the Brotherhood of the Rosy Cross in 1615.

Rosicrucianism, which, like Freemasonry, called for a new age of enlightened thinking and living, took root in several northern German principalities during the early seventeenth century. It had adherents and supporters at the highest levels of society, including Friederich, Count Palatine of the Rhine, who married Elizabeth, the daughter of James I of England, in 1613. Another Rosicrucian-minded member of the German aristocracy was Augustus, Duke of Brunswick and Lunenburg, who spent time in England at the court of King James and involved himself in Sir Francis Bacon's literary work. During and after the religiously motivated and devastating Thirty Years War in Europe, many Rosicrucians sought safe refuge in England, where some became involved in the emerging Masonic movement that had come south from Scotland with King James and his entourage.

Dee, perhaps motivated in part by the growing belief in the possibility of creating a New Jerusalem in the New World, urged his queen to support colonization efforts in North America. His fervour for the expansion of England's domain led him to coin the phrase "the British Empire." Some of his sea-going contemporaries, men also caught up in the liberated thinking of the time, set out to make it a reality.

Sir Francis Drake was a truly exceptional man in an age which seemed to breed his kind. Born of yeoman stock around 1545, he was blessed with an adventurous spirit. He was put to sea at an early age, perhaps in his teens, where he came under the tutelage of seasoned mariners. Drake acquired his learning and exceptional seafaring skills early in life from his mentor, Sir John Hawkins. He learned quickly that international piracy was commonplace and that English ships were obligated by national pride, religion and economic necessity to attack and raid the vessels of their enemies, especially those of the haughty and powerful Spanish, whose ships were often loaded down with gold, silver and gems from the American colonies. One of Drake's richest prizes was the capture of the *Carafuego* off the coast of Ecuador in 1579. Its cargo included twenty-six tons of silver, eighty pounds of gold, a dozen chests of coins, and a chart showing the hiding place of a treasure hoard on the isthmus of Panama. In his lifetime he captured more than one hundred Spanish ships. His audacity and stunning success at sea made him the envy of other commanders and caused the Spaniards themselves to exclaim in amazement that "were it not that he was a Lutheran, there was not the like man in the world."

Drake's extraordinary achievements contributed greatly to England's eventual rule over the waves. Following his triumphant and profitable circumnavigation of the globe in 1577-80, England hailed Drake as the boldest and bravest seaman of his age and the queen dined with him on his ship. He achieved still greater naval glory for his decisive role in routing the Spanish Armada in 1588. Drake, some of whose logs are still missing, even though they were turned over at court, crossed the Atlantic many times and was certainly familiar with the waters and coastlines of the Americas. Less-heralded exploits on the North American seaboard included his rescue of the half-starved remnants of Sir Walter Raleigh's first colony on Roanoke Island in Virginia. In 1586, after raiding Santo Domingo, he sailed northwards from the Caribbean with several ships, heading towards the coasts of Newfoundland and Labrador. On board were more than two hundred slaves which he intended to leave there along with some of the ships. What the purpose of that mission was nobody seems to know. Drake's achievements made him not only a wealthy national hero and a legend in his own lifetime but brought him to the attention of an adventurer of a different kind and perhaps the greatest Elizabethan of them all, Sir Francis Bacon.

In material sent to me by David Tobias, I discovered that Triton had received information from the Baconian societies in England and the United States confirming that Sir Francis Bacon and Drake had worked closely together at times and that Joachim Gaunse, Europe's most noted mining engineer at the time, and a group of Cornish miners had been shipped across the Atlantic by Drake. Nobody seems to know where they went or what they were up to during their sojourn in the New World. It is possible that Oak Island was explored at the time, its naturally formed caverns in the limestone bedrock discovered and used, or simply noted, as an ideal location to conceal and protect a treasure. If first found and utilized by Drake or Raleigh to hide captured Spanish gold, the island might later have been used by Bacon and his associates for long-term storage of valuable manuscripts.

Also known to have crossed the Atlantic was Thomas Bushell, a Bacon protegé and England's chief mining engineer during the reign of King Charles I. Bushell was an expert in the construction of underground water channels and the flooding and pumping out of mines. Again no record has ever been found of the purpose of his journey or of what he accomplished. His professional expertise, association with Bacon and involvement in the esoteric spiritual movement of his time makes him a likely candidate as the man who supervised the completion of the underground workings on Oak Island. If he was involved, it was almost certainly on behalf of his mentor and benefactor, Sir Francis Bacon.

Bacon, the lawyer, metaphysician, philosopher, scientist, writer, and statesman had more than a passing interest in the New World. He perceived it as offering an ideal opportunity and location for the development of a future idyllic state, a New Atlantis, and he was associated with a number of private enterprises involved in setting up colonies in North America. One such company was granted a colonization charter by King James I that is believed by some to have included the land mass then known as Acadia, which would have included Oak Island. He was also a close associate at court of the Scottish-born poet, philosopher and statesman Sir William Alexander, who helped found the first English settlement at Charlesfort in 1627 and gave Nova Scotia its name.

However, England's exploration of the New World had begun much earlier. Perhaps encouraged by Dee's persistent prodding and Drake's successes at sea, Elizabeth had eventually given her blessing and a colonial charter, but little else, to the adventurous Sir Humphrey Gilbert, who set sail from Plymouth in 1583 on a northerly route. His successful crossing and landfall had given Elizabethan England the island of Newfoundland and its first fragile colony in the New World. Gilbert earned himself a guaranteed place in history but lost his life in the process. His ship, *The Squirrel*, sank in heavy seas with all hands on board while on its way southwards past Nova Scotia in search of a more hospitable location. Gilbert's half-brother and one of Elizabeth's favourites at court, the talented and dashing Sir Walter Raleigh, inherited Gilbert's charter and was somewhat more successful. The queen, who had strong feelings of affection for the handsome and intelligent courtier, approved of Raleigh's transatlantic quests but kept him by her side.

After a first exploratory expedition failed to take root, Raleigh's second attempt in 1587 succeeded, at least temporarily. His people established a settlement much further south, the famous "Lost Colony" of Roanoke Island, Virginia, which Raleigh dutifully named after his admiring queen. Conflict between England and France interrupted Raleigh's colonization plans, and when supply ships returned to Roanoke Island a few years later, its inhabitants had mysteriously disappeared.

Raleigh, who fell out of favour with the queen because of his secret marriage to one of her ladies-in-waiting, focused his later maritime exploits in South America, where he took numerous risks trying to find the fabled wealth of El Dorado. Never popular with King James I, Raleigh underestimated the king's determination to keep the peace with Spain and to be rid of him. Following an unfortunate skirmish with the Spanish while on a second expedition up the Orinoco River in South America, he returned to England empty-handed. This accomplished adventurer and a man of letters was executed as a traitor in London in 1618.

With secrecy and intrigue a central part of the society in which Raleigh functioned, who knows what other exploits this free-spirited knight of the realm and contemporary of such men as Dee, Drake, Bacon and Alexander might have been involved in during his journeys into the unknown territories of the New World? He too could have been involved as a privateer or as an associate in a mission to ship a secret treasure to Oak Island.

Elizabeth did not live long enough to see the colonization dreams of some of her outstanding subjects realized. Within a few short years of her death, ships sent out by the privately operated Virginia Company of London, in which Sir Francis Bacon was a partner, sailed into Chesapeake Bay in 1608 and established the historic settlement of Jamestown, named after her successor, King James I. This small settlement formed the nucleus of a New England that was to grow and prosper alongside the American colonies of France and Spain. Eventually England's colonial child outgrew the other two, not only geographically but politically as well, due in part to the visionary and encouraging influence of Masonry and Rosicrucianism.

Given that the privateer Sir Francis Drake had sailed north from Florida with a shipload of slaves in the direction of Labrador, that the privately operated Virginia Company sent forces to Nova Scotia to oust the French from Port-Royal, and that the Northern Virginia Company, of which Bacon was also a part, shipped settlers as far north as Newfoundland, one can conclude that one or more of them could have been engaged in unreported activity involving Oak Island. And certainly there could have been other undocumented excursions up and down the eastern coast of North America by Elizabethan navigators during a time when the New World attracted the attention of individuals and groups interested in everything from the creation of a utopian society to searching for cities of gold.

If ever there was a time and place of political intrigue, religious turmoil, expanding knowledge and endless adventure, it was Elizabethan England. The poor and the pompous mingled to wonder at and enjoy the audacious spectacle and brilliance of the Shakespearean dramas. Under the perceptive gaze of a most learned if not eloquent queen ably served by astute advisers, England grew politically and culturally. Men as remarkable as her trusted secretary William Cecil, Lord Burghly; legislator Edward Coke; mathematician and cartographer John Dee; physicians William Harvey, William Gilbert and Robert Fludd; writer Ben Johnson; architect Inigo Jones; explorers Drake and Raleigh; the temperamental courtier Robert Devereux; and the all-embracing genius Francis Bacon all played their parts upon its expansive stage. But Elizabethan England was also a time of appalling social injustice, and towards the end of the queen's reign the country was seething with political and religious unrest. The average English person was overburdened with death-inducing toil, suffered from constant insecurity and poor food and saw little prospect of advancing themselves or their cause. Parliament was out to curb the power of the monarchy, and the Puritans were waiting in the wings.

It was a time heavily pregnant with the seeds of change, a time in which many set their sights on new horizons which included the newly discovered continents to the west. It was a time of turbulence and uncertainty in high places which spawned suspicion, secrecy and subterfuge. Conspiracies were everywhere, and the aging Elizabeth had good reason to be wary. The heavy machinery of state and church often combined to break the spirit and the bodies of those too impatient for change or considered too dangerous to the established order.

To some, the recently discovered continents across the sea offered safer if not better possibilities for progress. To Sir Francis Bacon, they offered the opportunity to advance his vision of a New Atlantis where his profound philosophy and scientific insights could flourish and his great literary masterpieces would be secure for future generations to appreciate.

17

A Playwright for Posterity

While studying English literature many years ago, I learned to view the plays attributed to William Shakespeare as works of great psychological and philosophical depth contained within compelling dramas and entertaining comedies. As an aspiring actor and playwright, I considered Shakespeare to be the definitive dramatist.

When I first came across the theory that Sir Francis Bacon (1561-1626) was the real author of the plays, I was naturally skeptical. But after studying the lives and work of both men, I have no doubt that Bacon was the playwright and William Shakspere (1564-1616), an actor and theatre manager from Stratford, his willing accomplice. This is a view shared by many researchers, including literary historians, writers, statesmen and psychologists. Apart from some suspicions when the plays were originally produced, the debate about their authorship first became a public issue in 1785 when the Reverend James Wilmot, who was interested in writing a biography, discovered that there was absolutely no evidence that the Stratford actor wrote anything, not even a letter to his long-suffering wife. He had little or no education, possessed no books and made no mention of literary works in his will. When he died in Stratford, he was not eulogized as a playwright.

One of the great mysteries of English literature is that the original manuscripts of the Shakespearean plays have never been found, and it has long been believed that they were purposely hidden in such a way and place that they would not be recovered for many centuries. In 1888, Ignatius Donnelly claimed to have discovered secret messages in the plays which revealed that Sir Francis Bacon was the real author. His book *The Great Cryptogram* created quite a storm in literary and academic circles at the time. The debate about the authorship of the plays has raged ever since and been the subject of many articles, debates, books, and radio and television programs. More recently the play "I, Prince Tudor, Wrote Shakespeare" by Norfolk-based American playwright Paula Fitzgerald was produced at the Library Theatre in Williamsburg, Virginia. In the play, Bacon

Portraits of (left) Sir Francis Bacon and (right) his alleged father, Robert Dudley, Earl of Leicester.

is presented as not only the disowned son of Queen Elizabeth but as a Christian visionary and the inspired writer of the Shakespearean plays.

In 1895, Dr. Orville Owen, an American Baconian scholar from Detroit published *Sir Francis Bacon's Cipher Story,* in which he expressed his conclusion that the original manuscripts were buried in a sunken vault in England. After locating the vault and finding it empty, he concluded that the valuable manuscripts had been taken out of the country. In 1901, Elizabeth Gallup, in *The Bilateral Cipher of Sir Francis Bacon*, confirmed Dr. Owens' revelations and fully explained her methodology for deciphering the code contained in the plays. In 1940, Dr. Burrell Ruth, a professor of chemical engineering at Iowa State University and another Baconian scholar, wrote to treasure hunter Gilbert Hedden expressing his belief that, based on discoveries made in the Pit and elsewhere on the island, it was likely that Bacon's manuscripts were part of the Oak Island treasure. According to Hedden's widow, her husband strongly believed in this possibility. Later, Nebraska lawyer Thomas Leary expressed the same conviction in his booklet entitled "The Oak Island Enigma," a copy of which I found in the files at the Nova Scotia Archives in Halifax. Bacon was known as an authority on secret cipher writing, much in use during his lifetime, and devoted a chapter to it in his *The Advancement of Learning*.

Apart from the discovery of the well-engineered workings and cryptic rock markings on Oak Island, traces of mercury and a piece of parchment with writing on it were found in the Pit. Ruth, in his letter to Hedden, pointed out that although liquid mercury was used in mining during the sixteenth century, it was also recommended by the scientifically inclined Bacon as a suitable agent for the long-term storage of manuscripts. Bacon, a persistent scientific experimenter, wrote about this theory in his renowned work *Sylva Sylvarum*.

Numerous bits of broken clay flasks that have traces of mercury have been found on the island. These, and an old leather shoe found elsewhere along the shoreline, have been determined to be of Elizabethan vintage. None of these discoveries by any means proves that the Oak Island treasure contains the missing original Shakespearean manuscripts, but they have opened the door to that possibility.

Naturally many questions have been asked as to why Bacon would have concealed his authorship of the plays. And why would he have arranged to hide the original manuscripts on a small island in the New World?

As mentioned, Queen Elizabeth I, in the interests of protecting her reputation and her throne, and encouraged by her wily chief adviser Sir William Cecil, Lord Burghley, refused to recognize or reward Francis Bacon as her son and heir. When the well-educated, travelled and exceptionally gifted Bacon began to write his inspiring and at times politically sensitive plays, works he wrote to educate and morally instruct his fellow countrymen and women through the entertaining medium of the theatre, he was admonished by both his foster father, Sir Nicholas, and the queen. Concerned about his future prospects at court, his personal security and the advancement of the plays, he sought out a suitable collaborator. This was a practice common among literary-minded members of the Elizabethan aristocracy. Bacon found his man in an up-and-coming actor from Stratford-upon-Avon by the name of William Shakspere, a name that approximated Bacon's own view of himself as a spear shaker for truth. Naturally, the one-time butcher's apprentice and stagehand was more than happy to participate in the scheme. The newly invented "Shakespeare" quickly gained a reputation as a brilliant playwright and, financed by Bacon, the plays were safely produced. Meanwhile, Bacon pursued his own rightful advancement at court, only to be frustrated at every turn by Lord Burghley and the queen herself. This briefly is the historical background to the Bacon-wrote-Shakespeare theory.

I was pleasantly surprised to discover that a good deal of the material sent to me by David Tobias in late 1993 and early 1995 focused on theories I myself had concluded were the most tenable. These involved Elizabethan England and the men of that era most likely to have been associated with Oak Island. Several references were made to Sir Francis Bacon and his associates, the explorer Sir Francis Drake and the innovative mining engineer Thomas Bushell. Reading through the material, it was obvious that the Oak Island Exploration Company gave credence to the Bacon-wrote-Shakespeare theory and the possibility of a conspiracy to bury the original manuscripts of the plays and other valuables on Oak Island.

In the detailed correspondence between Tobias and the Sir Francis Bacon Society in Surrey, England, and the Bacon Foundation in Claremont, California, various possibilities connecting Bacon to the Oak Island mystery were mentioned. These included: his prominent role as a member of the Virginia Company, responsible for fostering Jamestown in 1607 as well as other colonies and explorations in North America; a land grant from King James I which may have given Bacon and his associates access to Nova Scotia; Bacon's close working relationship with Sir William Alexander, the founder of Nova Scotia; and his interests in mining, underground water courses and the use of mercury for preserving manuscripts. In addition, reference was made to Bacon's Masonic and Rosicrucian-like philosophy, as expressed in his work *New Atlantis*.

It is generally accepted that Bacon was a leading light in the evolution of the sixteenth- and seventeenth-century esoteric spiritual movement of which Masonry and Rosicrucianism were part. Members of both practised the art of cryptic writing, by which they hid their secret teachings from the uninitiated and protected themselves from persecution. Bacon was known to have practised the art, and his influence on both esoteric organizations is readily recognized by their respective scholars and historians.

According to Christopher Nicolai, a Masonic writer of the late eighteenth century, Lord Bacon endeavoured through his work to bring about the regeneration of the world. One of his great undertakings was to demonstrate the essential order and beneficence of Creation with scientific proofs from nature. This idea he first promulgated in *Instauratio Magna* and later in *New Atlantis*. King Charles I of England was taken by the idea and had intended to pro-

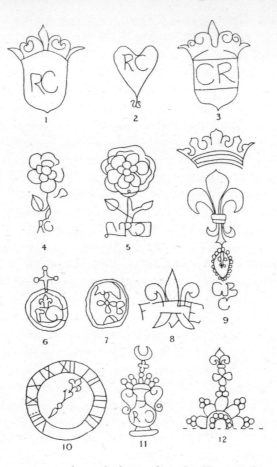

Rosicrucian watermark symbols used on Sir Francis Bacon's manuscripts.

mote something along these lines; unfortunately, civil war and his own execution put an end to the project. The idea lay dormant for some time but was subsequently revived in 1646 when several learned men founded the Royal Society in London for the purpose of carrying out Bacon's plan of communicating scientific and philosophical truths to the world.

The information provided to Tobias by Thomas Bokenham, chairman of the Bacon Society in England, contained details about Bacon's scientific interests and their obvious applicability to the man-made workings found on Oak Island. For instance, in *Sylva Sylvarum*, along with discussing the preservation of valuable manuscripts in mercury, Bacon had described the creation of artificial springs using stone, sand and ferns, a system somewhat similar to that found under the beach at Smith's Cove. Bokenham said Bacon was keenly interested in mining endeavours of all kinds and even foresaw the possibility of creating a huge underground storage and research facility. The correspondence also referred to Bacon's extensive use of cipher writing to secretly convey that he was the real author of the Shakespearean plays. The Oak Island Exploration Company is obviously well aware that Bacon had both the ability and the motive to create the Oak Island works.

Although Bokenham personally discounted the likelihood that the lost original manuscripts of the plays had been buried by Bacon or his associates in North America, preferring instead to believe that they remained in his own native England, he brought up the matter of the manual on cipher writing published in 1624 by Augustus, Duke of Brunswick and Lunenburg, in which coded messages concerning authorship of the plays are allegedly explained. Having come across a copy of this unique and fascinating publication among the rare Baconian Collection at Dalhousie University's Killam Library in Halifax, I was already aware of its potential significance in helping to solve the mystery surrounding the authorship of the plays, if nothing else.

Following the conference about the Oak Island mystery held at the Oak Island Inn at Western Shore in mid-October 1993, I wrote to Bokenham, anxious to know more about the secret messages Bacon was said to have coded into his writings and the applicability of the Duke of Brunswick and Lunenburg's *Cryptomenytices* to the problem of deciphering them. Bokenham's reply contained not only an explanation of the cipher system used by Bacon but also a startling interpretation, using the code explained in Augustus' book, of a coded message contained in one of the Shakespearean sonnets.

But Bokenham first made reference to lines delivered by the aging magician-philosopher Prospero, believed by some to be modelled on Francis Bacon or John Dee, towards the end of the play "The Tempest," itself set on a mysterious island, in which he says,

> I'll break my staff,
> Bury it certain fathoms in the earth,
> And deeper than did ever plummet sound
> I'll drown my book.

The implication was that these lines contained a veiled reference to Bacon's intention to bury his original manuscripts and other metaphysical writings in a deep, water-protected island site.

Then, after providing historical background to his own theory that the Oak Island treasure could possibly contain South American gold taken by Sir Walter Raleigh on his last western voyage in 1616, Bokenham went on to postulate that, because of their shared interest in Rosicrucian or Masonic matters, Raleigh may have informed Bacon of the treasure's whereabouts and it may have ended up as part of the entire cache on Oak Island. After reading about this possibility, I wondered whether the explorer involved may have been Drake rather than Raleigh.

However, what were of particular interest to me were comments made by Bokenham about the likelihood that Bacon's devotee and close associate, the mining engineer Thomas Bushell, may have executed the extensive underground workings found on Oak Island or extended some already created by Raleigh or Drake, both of whom were known to have used slave labour. Bushell's extensive knowledge of mining techniques and his closeness to Bacon made him the ideal man for the job, one that required professional know-how, efficiency and, above all, secrecy.

According to his biography, *The Superlative Prodigal*, Bushell was mystically inclined. His own comments reveal that Bacon encouraged him in his esoteric pursuits, shared his scientific knowledge and experimental research with him, helped him financially and finally entrusted to him his "dearest secret." Bokenham suggested that Bacon thereby charged Bushell with the reburial of the supposed Walter Raleigh treasure. However, my research into Bacon's life and the history of Masonry, its symbolism and mythology, led me to conclude otherwise.

The account of the instructions given to Bushell by Bacon was that he not use such "treasures as shall be gained thereby" in any way other than for "the raising, qualifying and endowing of my Solomon's House, modelled in my New Atlantis to my proposed ends, according to the duty of an obliged servant and faithful steward."

The reference to "Solomon's House" in "New Atlantis" is distinctively and clearly Masonic, as will be seen below in my chapter on the history of Freemasonry, and specifies the beneficial spiritual and moral purpose to which the treasure should be used. After

THE TREASURE IS ON
ISLE IN MAHONE BAY
OR
THOMAS BUSHELL'S
TREASURE ETC.

FRA TUDOR AUTHOR
NEW SCOTLAND ISLE

Messages deciphered from Shakespeare's Sonnet 52 by T.D. Bokenham. Baconia Magazine, *Fall 1993.*

Bacon's death, Bushell lived the life of a religious hermit for three years on a remote island off the west coast of England. During or shortly after this period as a recluse, Bushell is believed to have sailed across the Atlantic. It seemed to me that Bushell was involved in much more than the reburial of a supposed Raleigh treasure, and I came across definite indications of this in examples supplied by Bokenham of hidden messages he had deciphered from one of the sonnets, using a pre-established mathematical formula. These messages read "Fra Tudor Author" and "New Scotland Isle." The term *Fra Tudor* was one that had been used at times to refer to Bacon. A third message read "The treasure is on isle in Mahone Bay."

Of course, without spending a good deal of time carrying out detailed and exhaustive research into the cipher system said to exist in the plays, and short of finding the original Shakespearean manuscripts with his name on them, one cannot prove that Bacon was their author. This is a subject that requires and merits much more space than is possible in this book. Surprisingly, a good deal of resource material for such research is already present in Nova Scotia.

The Dalhousie Bacon Collection is the third largest collection of first editions by and about Bacon in the world and contains several publications dealing with the question of the authorship of the Shakespearean plays. There I came across several convincing arguments for the case that Francis Bacon wrote the plays and further confirmation that he was very much part of the esoteric spiritual fraternity in England and on the continent during his lifetime. There were several references to something I had already accepted as fact, that the plays themselves were written out of a desire to communicate and instruct others in immutable inner laws to which humanity and nature are bound.

The excesses of the Catholic inquisitions in Europe and the unstable political and religious climate in England, where the Puritans, who hated the theatre with a vengeance, were gradually gaining the upper hand, would have given Bacon cause for concern that his life's work would be destroyed unless it was safely hidden for a future and hopefully more enlightened generation to appreciate and benefit from. There are indications in Bacon's will and in later comments by his secretary, Dr. William Rawley, that this was so.

Given that Bacon's thought and writings were closely aligned with and influenced the emerging Masonic and Rosicrucian movements and that he was both philosophically and practically interested in developing colonies in North America, colonies which were themselves later politically and socially influenced by Masonic principles, it may be expected that Bacon would have sought to have his original manuscripts, which he believed to be in danger of being destroyed, transferred to the new continent.

At a time when there was only a small and insecure French presence on Acadia's more sheltered Fundy shore, it would have been easy for an English ship or two to sail unnoticed into Mahone Bay on the new continent's northeastern extremity, an area familiar to the colonization company to which Bacon belonged. The mission: to locate a predetermined and perhaps already secured hiding place for the long-term storage of his original manuscripts of the great dramas, considered by Bacon to be essential to the future evolution and welfare of humanity. It has been suggested that Bacon's loyal and dedicated secretary William Rawley, who was entrusted with Bacon's writings after his death, may have been involved with Bushell in hiding the original manuscripts of the plays on Oak Island.

This hypothetical scenario becomes an historical possibility when one considers the life, times and adventurous exploits of a Bacon associate, Sir William Alexander, the founder of Nova Scotia.

18

The First Nova Scotian

It was the erudite and philosophically minded Scottish nobleman William Alexander who set up the first English-speaking settlement in Nova Scotia in 1627 and gave the colony its name, flag and coat of arms. He was also closely connected to the reviving Masonic movement in both Scotland and England.

James I of England was of Scottish origin, and indeed had been King James VI of Scotland prior to accepting the offer of the English crown in 1603. Naturally, he responded favourably to a proposal put forward by his close associate, poet, philosopher and fellow Mason to establish a New Scotland on the American continent. Sir William Alexander had for some years perceived the possibility of creating a New Scotland in abandoned Acadia to match the colonies already established in the New World by Spain, France and England. In 1621, King James, equally enthusiastic about the scheme, granted his friend a charter which made him almost sovereign ruler of all lands in continental northeastern America between latitudes forty-three and forty-five degrees. Alexander, whose family claimed royal lineage, was an accomplished Latin scholar, so he quite naturally named his newly acquired kingdom Nova Scotia.

Born about 1567 at the family manor in Clackmannanshire, he was the only son of Alexander Alexander of Menstrie. Orphaned at an early age, he was brought up and privately educated by a grand uncle, James Alexander, the burgess of Stirling. Displaying an eager ability to learn, he attended the universities of Glasgow and Leyden and gained a reputation as a scholar. Because his family had land holdings within the earldom of Argyle, he was selected as travelling companion to the seventh earl and immersed himself in the cultures of France, Italy and Spain, whose art and languages he admired and learned. On returning to Scotland, he was presented at court by the grateful Argyle, and the shrewd king, appreciating scholarship when he saw it, immediately appointed him tutor to his young son, Prince Henry.

Alexander's passion for poetry and the publication of his early work "The Tragedy of Darius" brought him favourable attention

Sir William Alexander. (Courtesy of the New Brunswick Museum)

from the king. Respectful of Alexander's philosophical counselling as set out in poetical compositions entitled "Tragedies of the Monarchy," the king made Alexander part of his Scottish retinue at court soon after he ascended the English throne in 1604. Knighted by King James, with whom he collaborated on a translation of the Biblical Psalms, he was also appointed to the powerful office of

Master of Requests.

According to early seventeenth-century records of the Masonic lodge at Scone, the king, who had a strong philosophical streak, a well-known intellectual curiosity and literary leanings, had been inducted as a Mason there several years before he travelled south. James' master of works in Scotland, the man who oversaw the construction and maintenance of all royal buildings and enjoyed a closer and more secretive connection with the royal household, had been the venerable William Schaw, one of the most significant figures in the sixteenth-century revival of Masonry in Scotland.

The possible direct significance of all of this to the Oak Island mystery is the fact that Schaw was Scottish. His stated recognition of the important role of the Templar Sinclair family in the Scottish Masonic hierarchy indicates that he would have been familiar with the exploits of the surviving Knights Templar and would have known something about the 1398 Henry St. Clair voyage to Nova Scotia. He also was, through his position at the court of his Masonic brother King James VI of Scotland, soon to be James I of England, also a working associate of Sir William Alexander, with whom he would surely have shared his interest in and knowledge of Masonic lore and any passed-on information about Nova Scotia.

Schaw also probably had close associations with his English counterparts such as the Euclidian scholar and astrologer John Dee and the man who made all knowledge his province, Sir Francis Bacon. The heroic Elizabethan seafarers Sir Francis Drake and Sir Walter Raleigh were likely aware of, if not influenced to some degree by, the teachings of Dee and Schaw. Their transatlantic adventures and the successful establishment of a colony by Bacon and his associates at Jamestown would have encouraged Alexander in his desire to set up his own colony in the Americas.

The time in which these men lived was one in which many secret associations and collusions arose in response to the political and religious fermentations in both England and Europe. The fractious and often destructive nature of national and international events threatened the freedom and even the survival of whole segments of society at that time. A secret mission to the New World would certainly have been a considered option among members of the Masonic and Rosicrucian movements who saw themselves as the protectors and progenitors of knowledge they believed necessary for the advancement of the human race. What better place than the

Masonicly connected colony of Nova Scotia and a strategically placed and island-laden bay in the centre of its Atlantic coast?

Schaw, with the king's blessing, officially reaffirmed in 1600 the centuries-long patronage of the Sinclair family of Rosslyn to Scottish Masonry, thereby establishing tangible historical links between the medieval Order of the Knights Templar, the transatlantic exploits of Henry St. Clair, the teachings of Masonry, the Stuart throne and the New World. The final links in this historical chain were forged when King James appointed his respected servant Sir William Alexander to high offices and granted him the kingdom of Nova Scotia. Alexander's brilliant contemplative mind and his incorruptible character, and their common nationality and shared interest in Masonic esoterica, had made him a natural and close confidant of the king. Given a seat on the Scottish Privy Council in 1615, he had walked the corridors of power alongside such men as Lord Chancellor Francis Bacon. His discussions with his fellow philosopher undoubtedly involved much more than matters of state.

A central point in Alexander's career came in September 1621, five years before Bacon's death, when Alexander's abiding interest in setting up a colony came to fruition. The charter granted to him by King James I appointed Sir William Alexander hereditary "Lieutenant" of New Scotland, entitled him to explore, settle and develop much of the northeastern land mass of America and gave him authority to create laws, erect cities, hold courts, coin money, grant lands and mine minerals wherever and whenever he wished therein. It was a prodigious prize, perhaps more than his early Presbyterian upbringing would have ordinarily permitted him to expect, although he was not deterred from naming a large part of his newly acquired colony Alexandria. From what is known of his character and interests, this name was most likely born out of his desire to emulate the ideals and achievements of the ancient Egyptian city by the same name. According to Masonic historians, it was from the renowned Alexandrian school of philosophy that the Masonic Order derived many of its secret allegorical doctrines, rituals and symbols. The Order's secret Christian teachings were certainly known by Sir William Alexander, and by Sir Francis Bacon and King James.

Having been involved with Portuguese mining engineer Paulo Pinto and others in a gold and silver mining operation at Crawford Muir and Hilderston in his native Scotland, Alexander undoubtedly was interested in similar possibilities in Nova Scotia. As dedicated

as he was to the admirable principle of creating a self-sufficient settlement based on agriculture, fishing and fur trading, he also recognized that for the colony to grow and prosper other sources of
wealth had to be found. He may have sent a mining engineer such as
Thomas Bushell to Nova Scotia as part of one of the early expedi-
tions in search of an ideal settlement location and potential mineral
resources. Bushell, entrusted with Bacon's "dearest secret,"may
have used the Alexander voyages to Nova Scotia as an opportunity
to transport and hide his master's precious manuscripts on Oak
Island. In this he would most certainly have been assisted by
William Rawley, Bacon's trusted secretary.

Sir William knew that without sufficient and sustained funding
the colony could not survive its early years. The heroic experiment
undertaken by the French at Port-Royal was a stark example of failure to be adequately prepared and financed. The Crown, though
looking kindly on the enterprise, kept its coffers closed, and so Sir
William, apparently of his own choosing, added his own coin and
initially funded the project himself. However, with expedition costs
continually mounting, he soon called on some of his Scottish
brethren to help create the colony in Nova Scotia.

However, apart from Sir Robert Gordon, who agreed to colonize
Cape Breton, not much enthusiasm was shown on the home front.
Grim accounts of the treacherous North Atlantic and the unknown
lands beyond passed down over the years by Scottish fishermen had
sent a shuddering chill through those who had listened. Stories
derived from the legendary St. Clair voyage of 1398 may also have
given many reason to hesitate in taking up Alexander's offer to settle
on land so far removed from the peat-warmed hearth and the
heather-covered hill. Besides, other, better-paying adventures were
already available nearer to home, in the men-hungry armies of
Europe.

Eventually though, a few brave souls signed up and the enterprise was on its way. The first expedition sailed out of the mouth of
the river Dee in June 1622 and, after an interrupted passage, the ship
reached the coast of Nova Scotia in September. The exhausted passengers and crew were rudely welcomed to their new home by a vigorous northwester which blew them all the way back to
Newfoundland, where they sat out the winter in the safe confines of
St. John's harbour.

A second ship, the *St. Luke*, arrived the following spring and, after picking up the ten surviving members of the earlier voyage, passed down the uninhabited southeastern coast of Nova Scotia. From existing accounts we know it sailed close to Mahone Bay, as there is a mention of its crew and passengers going ashore not much farther to the south at Port Mouton. The shipmaster's record of the venture does not mention leaving anyone or anything on land, but there is also no reference to how long they remained in the area. Again, it is possible that a mining crew was set down on Oak Island or the nearby mainland, and the matter was kept secret for business, political or Masonic reasons.

After receiving positive accounts of the Nova Scotia terrain from members of his second expedition sent out in 1623, but by now being heavily in debt, Alexander appealed to the king, who had associated himself with the venture to the extent of having his portrait affixed alongside Sir William's on the original charter. Between them they devised a plan to attract other able men to the venture. In 1624, King James I announced his intention to create the regal Order of the Baronetage of Nova Scotia. In a letter to the Privy Council dated October 18, 1624, James declared that "the whole Scottish nation would derive profit from the settlement" and that he was "so hopeful of the enterprise and intend to make it a work of my own."

In researching the facts surrounding Sir William Alexander's several attempts to colonize Nova Scotia, one encounters a dramatic lack of detail and several frustrating contradictions. For instance, although hard pressed for money, Sir William fitted out yet another vessel, *The Eagle*, in March 1627, but it failed to sail and lay idly at anchor in the Thames for almost a year. Meanwhile, his eldest son, also named William, was away on a mysterious voyage during which, according to conflicting accounts, he either commanded a squadron of ships on a privateering adventure against a French fleet off the shores of Nova Scotia or participated in an altogether different expedition with Sir David Kirke in the St. Lawrence region. Still another account has him arriving in Port-Royal in early 1627 and setting up his own colony there. It is interesting to note that following his return he demonstrated a new-found wealth, making a large donation to the poor of Stirling. Did he uncover part of a Spanish treasure hidden years earlier by Drake or Raleigh on Oak Island?

With the ambitious Cardinal Richelieu showing renewed interest in Acadia and forming his Company of One Hundred Associates to set up additional fur-trading outposts in New France, Alexander realized he had to put settlers down somewhere in Nova Scotia soon or risk losing it altogether. The pressing problem of financing yet another attempt, larger and better equipped than the others, was resolved with help from his former pupil and new king, Charles I. Like his deceased father, Charles expressed wholehearted enthusiasm for Alexander's visionary plans to extend Scotland's name and fame on the other side of the Atlantic. Not only did he renew the original charter, but he caused the Scottish treasury to cough up a large sum to alleviate the ever-mounting cost.

One source states that in 1628 four heavily laden ships with many skilled craftsmen, their families and necessities on board struck out for the new land. They arrived unhindered by either the French or the weather, and under the command of Alexander's eldest son, William, set themselves to the task of creating a new home in the attractive wilderness in and around the former site of Port-Royal, rechristened Charlesfort after the new English king.

Although King Charles I publicly expressed support for the project, suggesting that it could be an outlet for Scottish enterprise, provide new opportunity for labour and increase the prosperity of the nation as a whole, some members of the established Scottish aristocracy were opposed to Alexander's plan. In 1630 Alexander used his literary talents to write a long article entitled "Encouragement to Colonies." Accompanied by a map of the geographical area involved, which included part of present-day Quebec, Maine, New Brunswick, Nova Scotia, and Prince Edward Island, the article encouraged other Scottish nobles to participate by passionately appealing to their sense of moral duty, spirit of adventure and desire to advance their standing in the world. Over one hundred responded, but not even their participation could save Alexander's colony.

Alexander's hope of creating a new domain in Nova Scotia was crushed when the war ended and the Treaty of Saint Germain-en-Laye of 1631 specified that all occupied properties in the New World previously claimed by the French were to be returned to them. In spite of Sir William Alexander's efforts to convince the king not to forfeit Charlesfort and his prized colony of Nova Scotia, Charles did just that.

Alexander was ordered to demolish Charlesfort and return all the people and their possessions to Scotland. Even if Oak Island had not already been utilized during the colonization attempts, it is possible that, before departing Nova Scotia, the Alexanders hid Masonic documents and others valuables entrusted to them on the island. They may have expected that their political fortunes would change and they would soon be returning to the previously explored island, far enough away from French interests at Port-Royal to be considered safe.

By 1632 Alexander's vision of a New Scotland lay shattered even though the king assured him that the Nova Scotia charter still stood. By way of compensation, Charles gave Alexander a promissory note for ten thousand pounds, which proved uncollectable, and a new grant of land in New England. Displaying an indomitable spirit of patient perseverance in adversity, a spirit that later Nova Scotians would often emulate, he returned to his love affair with the Muse and devoted his talents during his remaining years to the duties of his many public offices.

In spite of being appointed Earl of Stirling and Viscount Canada, financial troubles and a deep sorrow swept away the peace of his final days. His two eldest sons, William and Anthony, an architect and the king's master of works, who had participated with him in the Nova Scotia project, died early deaths within a year of each other. Creditors hounded Alexander until he died insolvent in 1640. But this noble Scottish statesman, although deprived of material good fortune at home and overseas, nonetheless left a rich legacy. His dedicated work as an official of the realm and as a colonizer, poet and philosopher left a mark upon the skein of time and influenced the hearts and minds of those who followed. Admired by his fellow literati at home and abroad, Alexander's expansive learning and pro- lific output earned him a notable place in the annals of Scottish liter- ature. His contemporary William Drummond referred to him in his biography as a "man among men" and the "poet of Agincourt." His collected works published a few years before his death in 1640 and entitled *Recreations with the Muses* display his preoccupation with the deeper currents of thought of his age. His varied compositions, not surprisingly, contain an addition to Sidney's unfinished work on the legendary idyllic land of Arcadia.

There could hardly have been a more just and nobler first Nova Scotian than Sir William Alexander. In commemoration of his con- tribution to the history of this land, a cairn of solid Scottish stone stands in silent witness upon the grass at the corner of busy South Park Street and University Avenue in Halifax. Sadly ironic is the fact that the French and English who made the two first courageous attempts to develop permanent settlements in Nova Scotia eventually fell victim to political events beyond their control.

The records of Masonry in Scotland show that the Alexander family was closely connected to the Edinburgh Lodge, considered by many Masons to be the oldest in Scotland. Among the few remaining early records of this lodge, which had close connections to the Crown, is mention that on July 3, 1634, both William Alexander Jr. and his younger brother Anthony were initiated as members. In February 1638 another Alexander brother, Henry, who succeeded Anthony as the king's master of works, was also admitted. From what is known about the interests of their father and his associations at court and with other intellectuals and creative minds of his day, it is safe to assume that he also was involved in Masonic activity, in his native Scotland and in London. He was certainly an exponent in his poetry and public life of many of Freemasonry's beliefs and aspirations.

That being the case, it becomes distinctly possible that his plans for Nova Scotia were inspired more by his Masonic ideals and principles than by any desire to profit personally. The facts that he used his own money to get the project under way and expressed a high-minded approach to developing it confirm that this venture was not embarked upon purely for personal gain and glory, if at all. Associated as he was with high-ranking members of the Masonic organization in both England and Scotland, and given Masonry's revered practice of secrecy, it is not stretching the line too thin to postulate that, should there have been a reason to remove precious inner-circle possessions out of the country, Alexander was the ideal man for the job and his colony the perfect place for the concealment. Never was there a more perfect set of circumstances for the secret shipment of Bacon's original manuscripts to Nova Scotia than during the time of Sir William Alexander.

19

Masonic Connections

My research led me to the Nova Scotia Public Archives in Halifax, the library of the *Chronicle-Herald* newspaper, Dalhousie University and the Grand Lodge of Nova Scotian Masons. At the Archives, I was completely surprised by the quantity of material on Oak Island, much of it donated by Reginald Harris, which consists mostly of his and Frederick Blair's accumulated information, confirming in precise detail aspects of the searches they had been involved in. There are numerous letters, diagrams and newspaper clippings, and among the papers are many scribbled notes made by Harris to himself for future reference, presumably with his book in mind.

Much of Harris's material was written on Masonic letterhead, and at least one meeting related to Oak Island business had been held in the Masonic Hall on Barrington Street in Halifax, where Harris, as secretary of the Fraternity, occupied an office. One person present at that meeting had been Dr. Frederick Hamilton, past Grand Master of the Grand Lodge of Massachusetts and Oak Island treasure hunter between 1938 and 1944. Harris himself had been Grand Master of Scotia Masons from 1932 to 1935, and Oak Island owner Mel Chappell had also held that office between 1944 and 1946. Blair, who had been connected with the Oak Island treasure search for almost sixty-five years, also held Masonic office. I would later discover that many of the other prominent figures involved in the Oak Island treasure search over the years have likewise been members of Masonic lodges.

Some of the notes I found mentioned that, in 1936, Gilbert Hedden had found pieces of an inscribed stone on the north end of the island. Although the writing looked very old, Hedden seemed to attach no importance to it, apparently considering it a hoax. I also found a note in which Harris made mention of three large piles of stones found on the high ground on the east end of the island.

Then there was a well-worn copy of a small, privately published book entitled *The Oak Island Enigma*. Its author, Thomas P. Leary, drawing on the conclusions of Baconian scholar Dr. Burrell Ruth of

Iowa in 1939, put forward the theory that Oak Island contained a vault in which the long-lost original Shakespearean manuscripts were hidden. Central to this theory was Bacon's research into the ability of mercury to preserve manuscripts for long periods of time. Clipped to the book's cover was Harris's record of a statement made to Hedden in 1937 by a workman named Baker that specks of liquid mercury had been seen on the drill bit on one occasion as it was extracted from the depths of the shaft. This formed the basis for Hedden's belief that the Pit might actually contain the missing Shakespearean manuscripts.

After noting and confirming that several of the key figures involved in the Oak Island search over the years were high-ranking members of the Masonic Order in Canada and the United States, I decided to explore the possible implications. I was convinced that, given the connections implied by the inscribed stones, stone markers, cryptic writings and cross, the involvement of key Masonic figures was more than coincidence.

Although I had acquired a general understanding of the origins and aims of the Masonic Order over the years, I had never been a practising Freemason. Much has been written in recent years about the role played by the powerful Templar and Masonic organizations in political, social and cultural developments in Europe and North America over the centuries. Some loose connections have even been made to Oak Island and the surrounding area that involve the Knights Templar and their reputed missing treasure; it has been inferred that either the Holy Grail, the cup used by Jesus at the Last Supper, or the Ark of the Covenant, the container of the tablets on which the Ten Commandments were written, were part of this treasure.

If part of the Templar treasure, which is supposed to have disappeared with a Templar fleet from the port of La Rochelle in 1314, had been buried on Oak Island in Mahone Bay, symbolic markings would logically have been left on the island. Alternatively, if the 1398 voyage of Prince Henry St. Clair or the 1623 voyage of Sir William Alexander, both of whom were intimately connected to the Templar/Masonic/Rosicrucian movement, had led to the selection of Oak Island as a long-term repository of sacred treasure, symbolic indications would also have been in order. Given the intimate historical and philosophical connection between the Templars and Freemasons, some leading members of the groups associated with the Oak Island search during the past two hundred years must have clued into this fact.

Of course, the Masonic code of secrecy and their respect for anything to do with the Order's learned past would have prevented them from revealing, except among themselves, what they suspected lay buried on Oak Island. Even if no record, written or oral, existed within the Order of a Masonic treasure on this side of the Atlantic, they would certainly have been tipped off by the hieroglyphic writing, stone markings and other symbols found on the island. No wonder the publishers of the first book about the search for the treasure made pointed reference to author Reginald Harris's Masonic affiliation and suggested it might have a bearing on the mystery.

Given the rapid spread of Freemasonry among the citizenry in established centres in Nova Scotia during the fifty years after Cornwallis opened a Masonic Lodge in Halifax, it is almost a certainty that the organizers of the first coordinated dig—men such as the educated, affluent and well-connected Simeon Lynds, Colonel Robert Archibald, Captain David Archibald and Sherrif Thomas Harris—were Masonicly associated. Following the revelation of the unusual nature of the Pit, and especially after viewing the hieroglyphically inscribed stone, it is inconceivable that one of these men at least did not realize the possibility of a Masonic connection to the Oak Island treasure.

Successive treasure hunts throughout the past two hundred years often involved men who were prominent members of Masonic lodges. Some had passed through the higher levels of initiation, and a few even held the highest office possible within the Fraternity.

A.O. Creighton, treasurer of the Oak Island Association in 1866, who along with Jefferson McDonald took the cryptically inscribed stone off Oak Island to his bookbinding store in Halifax, was a Mason and must have had some sense of the origins of the mysterious markings on its face, even though their full meaning would have been known only by someone versed in the ancient art of cryptic writing. The gradual erosion of the inscription and the eventual disappearance of the stone itself may have been intentional. Of course, it is also possible that sheer ignorance of its real significance is what led to its loss.

One man with a long involvement with the Oak Island treasure search who collected and coordinated much of its checkered history until his death in 1951 was Frederick Blair. Personally associated with the Oak Island treasure search since 1893, with family connections to the enterprise going back as far as 1863, Blair was a prominent member of the Alexandra Lodge in Amherst. Amherst was also home to key figures such as Jefferson McDonald and William Chappell, men closely associated with Blair. It was Blair, along with Captain Welling, who first discovered the equilateral stone triangle, a Masonic symbol, on the south shore of the island in 1897.

Both William Chappell and his son Melbourne, who ended up owning much of the island in 1950, were active Freemasons. In fact, Mel Chappell was appointed Provincial Grand Master for Nova Scotia from 1944 to 1946, an office previously held by Reginald Harris between 1932 and 1935. Chappell retained an interest in the operation even after he sold his holdings on the island to Montreal millionaire David Tobias in the mid-1970s, and the Chappell family is still involved in the treasure search.

The independently wealthy Gilbert Hedden of Chatham, New Jersey, who carried out the treasure search from 1934 to 1938, and Professor Edwin Hamilton, who succeeded him and operated on the island for the next six years, were also Freemasons. Hamilton had at one time held the office of Grand Master of the Grand Lodge of Massachusetts. Hedden even made it his business to inform Mason King George VI of England about developments on Oak Island in 1939, and Hamilton corresponded with President Roosevelt, another famous Freemason directly associated with the mystery.

The fact that, for much of the past two hundred years, the Oak Island treasure hunt has attracted a continual stream of influential and high-ranking members of the Masonic Order does not necessarily point to organized conspiracy. But it does indicate a continual and committed interest in the mystery among members of the Fraternity. Many of these men involved themselves almost to the point of near financial ruin in their endeavours to solve it. When forced to abandon their attempts, some still kept close ties with the ongoing search. It is possible that something other than ego or the prospect of financial reward was behind such obsession. Perhaps they were only too aware that a treasure of great significance to the ancient Fraternity lay buried on Oak Island.

To understand the motive that might have driven these men to risk all—profession, family, reputation, health and even life itself— in pursuit of a mysterious and elusive treasure, I needed to understand more about the origin and nature of Freemasonry. This posed a challenge because, for so long, little genuine information has been openly available about Masonry. Over the years I had picked up only a few general details about the Order's past and purpose and its use of ritual and symbolism.

Fortunately, while taking a break from my Oak Island research, I came across several volumes of Masonic history in the private library of a house I was visiting in Ontario. Later, following a lecture I gave to a Masonic gathering about the possible connection between the Oak Island mystery and the Fraternity, Richard Fletcher of Washington, D.C., put me in touch with the Nova Scotia Lodge's past grand master Frank Milne, who arranged access for me to the Order's extensive library at the Grand Lodge on Barrington Street in Halifax. In turn, General Secretary Gerry Vickers proved a most willing and helpful source of information and took steps for me to receive access to the Masons' rarely seen files in the Public Archives.

Shrouded in secrecy for centuries, the Craft had allowed a mystique to evolve around itself. By the very fact that it preserves and practices secret rites, the Fraternity has attracted suspicion and even condemnation over the years from others who have had little real understanding of its aims.

Throughout history its membership has included royalty, clergy, intellectuals, artists, scientists, businessmen, merchants and military personnel of every nationality and religious persuasion. It is, I think, unfortunate that, in the glare of repeated adverse publicity resulting from some wrongdoing by one of its members or lodges, Freemasonry has for the most part remained silent concerning its high ideals, meaningful rituals and world-wide beneficence. Shriners notwithstanding, few members of the public are even aware of its existence, let alone its activities. This is in one sense a tribute to the Masons' loyal adherence to their rigid code of secrecy which, originated for good reason in antiquity, has enabled the Order to carry on its work for the most part undisturbed and unnoticed by the rest of society and to remain active in spite of sensational accusations being levelled against it from time to time.

If there is a Masonic connection to the Oak Island mystery, and I believe there is, then the centuries-old code of secrecy would also help explain how the extensive plan was implemented and kept quiet for centuries.

Secrecy and even subterfuge have been part of the Oak Island search at various times, although this may have more to do with the greed, fear and suspicion often associated with treasure hunts. Treasure hunting by its very nature often requires those involved to maintain a high degree of secrecy. Of course, assuming some of the early Oak Island Masonic treasure hunters suspected they were on the trail of something of immense importance to themselves as Masons, to their brotherhood and to humanity in general, it is understandable that they would want to protect their interests from outsiders while conducting their affairs as normally as possible.

The potential scope of the Oak Island mystery and the possibility of discovering something other than buried gold is implied in the opening paragraph of the present Oak Island Exploration Company's background material, faxed to me by company president David Tobias in April 1993:

> As you know, the founding members of Triton Alliance Ltd. are not treasure hunters per se vis-à-vis sunken ships, salvaging, etc. Our group is composed primarily of businessmen and professionals. . . . Our involvement is predicated on our field findings and their analyses, and especially the archaeological and historical implications which seem to be far reaching. Again, how often in a lifetime does one have the opportunity of being associated with one of the few great mysteries?

Thus I was not greatly surprised to learn that one of the company's principal researchers is Richard Nieman, a man who has also been involved with the Shroud of Turin project.

Some of the unusual discoveries made at Oak Island both on and below the ground are indicative of a possible religious connection to the treasure. These include the cryptically inscribed stone found in 1805 in the Pit and the large stone cross revealed by Fred Nolan in 1992. Several of the symbols found on the inscribed stone are sacred to Masons and Christians in general; others have been described as either Egyptian or Hebraic. The Cross, the circle with a central dot and the triangle all have deep spiritual significance for Freemasons. The symbolic inscription, although never photographed as far as we know, was written down by a retired Mahone Bay schoolteacher some ten or more years prior to the stone's final disappearance. In the late 1970s, the chief archivist of the Nova Scotia Archives sent a copy of this drawing to Dr. Barry Fell, a noted cryptologist formerly with Harvard University and author of several books on pre-European settlements in North America.

After examining the inscription, Fell concluded that it had a spiritual significance and was derived from a Middle Eastern form of writing used by an early Christian sect known as the Copts. Its message was to the effect that the people needed to remember their God or else they would perish.

Regardless of whether they would agree with this particular interpretation, many of the treasure hunters and present-day researchers have concluded that this inscribed stone probably was the key to a safe retrieval of the treasure. When I first read that this important piece of the Oak Island puzzle, which must surely have aroused the interest of the Masons involved in the search up to that time, had been allowed to disintegrate or disappear in Halifax, I accepted it as an unfortunate accident. However, after reading about the apparently intentional disappearance of the Port-Royal Masonic stone in Toronto around 1876, I naturally became more skeptical. In the case of the Port-Royal stone, on which the Masonic symbols of the square and compass and the date 1606 had been visible, several prominent Freemasons were involved, including Nova Scotia's own Judge Thomas Haliburton; Sir Sandford Fleming, the railway builder, inventor of standard time and the founder of the Royal Canadian Institute; and Sir Daniel Wilson, one of the institute's presidents.

Another interesting thing about the Oak Island stone was that it was olive-tinged granite or porphyry and, according to some who saw it, unlike any stone ever seen before in Nova Scotia.

Then there were the reports of strange markings on the base of a nearby tree and on the flat beach stones found on the wooden floor at the fifty-foot level of the Pit. There is no record of what these markings looked like, but it's reasonable to assume they resembled those on the slab found at the ninety-foot level.

The layers of charcoal, putty-like clay and a fibrous substance found at various levels in the Pit originally seemed to be of no apparent symbolic significance. I, like many, assumed they had performed the purely practical function of helping to seal or preserve the various wooden platforms. However, during my research into Masonic symbolism, I came across an interesting entry in Albert Mackey's *Encyclopaedia of Freemasonry* under the triple heading of

Chalk, Charcoal and Clay. These three substances were described as representing freedom, fervency and zeal, respectively, attributes recommended to the life of an Entered Apprentice Mason during his initiation.

I also discovered that the Pit itself, with its various levels and its deeply hidden treasure contained in a vault or cavern, has Masonic ritualistic connotations. Within Christian Masonry is a branch known as the "Cryptic Rite," or "Masonry of the Secret Vault," which stems from a mixture of legend and historical facts concerning a secret vault under King Solomon's Temple in Jerusalem that was said to contain important religious treasures. This rite also draws inspiration from the fact that initiation and education into ancient mysteries almost always took place underground or in an enclosed chamber, as in Egypt. The same practice was adopted by some early Christians.

The great doctrine taught in the mysteries was resurrection from the dead, so it was deemed proper to duplicate the process during initiation by entering into a subterranean vault representing the death of the physical and the birth of the spiritual. In the ancient mysteries, the vault was symbolic of the grave, and initiation was symbolic of death, where Divine Truth was to be found. The Masons adopted this practice in their Cryptic Rite rituals. I do not mean to suggest for a moment that Oak Island was at any time used as a site of initiation, Masonic or otherwise, but rather that one can find the use of Masonic symbolism in the construction of the vault-containing Pit.

The large equilateral triangle, each side ten feet long and made of beach stones, which Captain Welling discovered on the south shore of the island in 1897 is another major Masonic symbol, and one that Welling and Blair, as Masonic brothers from Amherst, must have attached some significance to, even though we are led to believe otherwise. Mackey's Masonic *Encyclopaedia* says no other symbol is more generally diffused throughout the whole system of Freemasonry than the triangle. The equilateral triangle, says Masonic writer D.W. Nash, "viewed in the light of those who gave it currency as a divine symbol, represents the Great First Cause, the creator and container of all things."

According to Reginald Harris, the triangle on the island was ignored for forty years until it was "rediscovered" by Gilbert Hedden, himself a Mason, in 1937. Hedden, we are told, attached importance to it only because it approximated one of the markings on a treasure map said to have belonged to Captain Kidd. However, there is no doubt that he too would have been aware of its possible Masonic significance, assuming he was receptive to that line of investigation. Laverne Johnson, a Mason from Vancouver, whom Elizabeth Sovie of Chester helped to relocate the neglected stone triangle in 1959, found an incised cross on its apex. Johnson then used the triangle to develop his own theory about the location of treasure, which he believes lies in shallow ground just northwest of the Pit.

While carrying out his detailed survey of the island, Fred Nolan came across two triangles formed by four very large piles of stones on the high ground north of the Pit. Another triangle, made up of five stones, was found close to a shoreline near the east end of the island in 1972. The fact that several stone triangles have been found in different locations on the island is, I believe, indicative that the people who left them there were familiar with the use of this shape for reasons other than directional. One organization thoroughly familiar with the symbolic use of the triangle is Freemasonry.

While scouring the island for other evidence, Hedden came across a large granite rock with letters engraved on it, half buried in the beach at Joudrey's Cove, obviously part of a larger rock. After describing this discovery to some of his workmen, one told him a huge boulder with strange markings on it had been found on the beach about fifteen years earlier but had been dynamited in the hope of finding treasure underneath it. However, there was no treasure, and many pieces of the marked stone were taken away as souvenirs.

Hedden immediately set up a search party which resulted in the discovery of a major piece of the original boulder that weighed several hundred pounds and bore markings unusual to anyone not familiar with sacred symbology. Here again, the Cross, the symbol of Christ, is centred between two other well-known Masonic markings, the letter H and a circle with a central dot. The large H is believed by some Masonic scholars to be a modification of the Hebrew letter for God or Jehovah, and the dot within the circle represents humanity within the fullness of God's Creation, or the individual Mason within his lodge.

In 1967, Dan Blankenship, as field manager of the newly formed Triton Alliance, carried out his own extensive search on the island. Among several interesting items he dug up from three feet below the beach at Smith's Cove was a heart-shaped stone, another prominent

Masonic symbol. This stone was submitted for examination to Mendel Peterson, the former curator of historical archaeology with the Washington-based Smithsonian Institution. Peterson, who has described Oak Island as one of the most fascinating archaeological sites in North America, concluded that the heart-shaped stone had been handworked with a sharp tool and was quite old. A second heart-shaped stone was found by Fred Nolan on his property.

In modern Masonic iconography the heart occupies a prominent position. It is an emblem associated with the third-degree ritual of initiation for a Master Mason. The symbolic meaning is that to be a full Mason one must be prepared in one's heart. According to the eighteenth-century German Masonic scholar and historian Carl Krause, the heart symbolizes the internal principle of Masonry, which addresses not only outward conduct but the inner spirit. The heart is also one of the dominant symbols of Rosicrucianism and is, of course, central to the Christian doctrine of universal love.

The G stone dislodged by a bulldozer east of the Pit in 1967 is another obvious example of Masonic symbolism. According to Blankenship, who cleaned the stone after its discovery, the large, chiselled-out letter had been on the side buried in the earth. Assuming the marking is authentic and not a hoax (the Oak Island operation offering plenty of incentive for falsifying evidence), this stone would leave little doubt that there is a sacred aspect to the treasure. In Masonic symbolism the letter G signifies the supremacy of God, the Grand Geometrician, as the focal point of all Masonic teachings. Prominently displayed on the eastern wall or entrance of every Masonic lodge and suspended over the Master Mason's chair, it is the most public and familiar of all symbols in Freemasonry. According to the eighteenth-century Masonic writer William Hutchinson, the letter G "denotes Geometry, which to artificers is the science by which all their labours are calculated and formed; and to Masons contains the determination, definition and proof of the order, beauty and wonderful wisdom of the power of God in his creation."

The presence of this symbol on Oak Island and its location in the east, seen as the source of light in Masonic teachings, is further indication that individuals with a fundamental knowledge of Freemasonry were likely involved.

The enormous stone cross discovered by Fred Nolan, which is also comprised of several smaller right-angle geometric formations, is the most significant symbolic structure found on Oak Island. Dr. Mudie's conclusion in October 1993 that the cross was man-made and that its boulders likely came from elsewhere on or off the island left no doubt in my mind that it is a new and major clue to understanding the nature of the Oak Island mystery. This gigantic and easily recognized symbol could have been left to indicate to others perhaps centuries later that the activity that once took place on Oak Island was related to Christianity.

In a fourteenth-century Masonic manuscript known as the "Halliwell Constitution" the origin of the Cross as a Masonic symbol is traced back through the ecclesiastically connected medieval guilds to the Gnostic Christians and beyond. An ancient and universal symbol of eternal life, it is used in the higher degrees, or levels of initiation, in Masonry and Rosicrucianism to represent the life, death and resurrection of Jesus Christ as a pattern for others to follow.

While unearthing a large uniformly shaped stone pile, which he believes may mark the concealed entrance to the underground workings, just northeast of the cross in 1993, Nolan also discovered that the top centre stone had a small cross cut into it.

Nolan also found an artifact nearby that has deep symbolic significance: a very old metal lock with a key in the form of a cross. On turning the key, the lock face opens to reveal yet another keyhole.

Even allowing that some tampering may have been done over the years with stones on Oak Island, it is highly unlikely that all of these structures and markings were executed and put in place by pranksters. The labour involved would have been immensely time-consuming. It is, I think, sufficiently obvious that sacred symbolism was used by those who carried out the original work.

The combined use of secrecy and religious symbolism in the creation of the Oak Island enigma, the extensive and intricate nature of the project, the time-frame scientifically established for its origin and the direct involvement of many high-ranking Freemasons in attempts to solve it makes a credible case for the theory that there is a Masonic/Rosicrucian connection to the mystery.

20

Secrets of Freemasonry

If there is, as I believe, a Masonic/Rosicrucian connection to the ingeniously hidden and protected Oak Island treasure, and if symbolic stone markers and writings were left to direct others to its location and retrieval, then some understanding of Freemasonry's origins, aims and achievements is required for a full appreciation, and perhaps a satisfactory conclusion, of this remarkable mystery.

Many branches of modern Freemasonry draw heavily upon the history, structure and symbology of the medieval guild of stone masons who built many of the visually stunning cathedrals and other remarkable buildings still standing in Europe today. There is a direct link between much of modern Freemasonry world-wide and the Grand Lodge established in London in 1717, but the fundamentals of Masonic philosophy go much further back and originate from a more universal source. Freemasonry and its associated order of Rosicrucianism are spiritually motivated fraternities that aim to improve the thinking and actions of their members and foster a heightened sense of service to others. Freemasonry relies heavily on sacred symbolism and legend and employs secret and at times flamboyant rituals of initiation.

The voluminous but rarely seen histories of Freemasonry provide evidence that many of the key figures in the setting up of English, Scottish and French colonies on the North American continent in the seventeenth century were active members of this expansive esoteric organization. Detailed records reveal the spread of Masonry through the lodge system and the growth of its membership during the early years of colonization. Almost the inevitable result of a natural, if at times tumultuous, political and social evolution, both the first prime minister of Canada, John A. Macdonald, and the first president of the United States, George Washington, were high-ranking Freemasons, and several of the founding fathers of both nations belonged to the Fraternity.

In Europe, the years between 1550 and 1650 were a time of dynamic cultural, political and religious forces that produced and emerged from the Renaissance and the Reformation, a time of unprecedented interest in arcane secrets and esoteric spiritual traditions. Students of the hidden knowledge of humanity believed that once they mastered its secrets and applied its teachings, then their world, victim to seemingly endless political and religious conflicts, would experience a truly enlightened age. At the very least, such mastery would alleviate some of society's ills.

During those centuries a large number of leading figures in many fields of human endeavour believed in the perfectibility of the earthly condition through a full development of human faculties and an understanding of the laws of nature, and many were actively committed to bringing it about through their endeavours in art, science and philosophy. Amidst this creative ferment, which reached a peak in England during the era spanning the reigns of Queen Elizabeth I and King James I, modern Freemasonry and Rosicrucianism evolved.

The society of medieval master masons, who built the great cathedrals of Europe and brought their cherished architectural skills and secret lore to England and Scotland, presented a natural foundation upon which William Schaw, the king's master builder and student of arcane knowledge, was able to establish a structured esoteric spiritual organization in Edinburgh in 1599. Speculative, or symbolic, Masonry owed its philosophical roots to the mystical Christianity of the Middle East which had been reintroduced in Europe in part through the activities of the twelfth-century military order of the Knights Templar. By the early seventeenth century, Masonry was already meshing with the *Rosicrucian Enlightenment* in England under the influence of men such as German philosopher and writer Johann Valentin Andrea and Queen Elizabeth's astrologer John Dee. During the first half of the seventeenth century this evolving esoteric movement attracted and was enlarged by men such as Francis Bacon, Robert Fludd, William Alexander and Inigo Jones in England, and Friederich, Count Palatine of the Rhine, and Augustus, Duke of Brunswick and Lunenburg, in Germany.

The result was that a previously underground movement, which in England now included artists, philosophers, scientists, statesmen and even monarchs, gained a reasonable measure of social and political acceptance and branched out into several avenues of expression. One was the establishment by Robert Moray, Elias Ashmole and others of the Royal Society in London in 1660. The movement's influence was noticeable in the arts, in the plays of Shakespeare and in architecture. By the beginning of the eighteenth century, it had found its way into the highest levels of English society and the nation's military command and was spreading through the political system and among the merchant class.

Out of a perceived need for a central governing body to regulate and coordinate the Order's expanding activity and assure its future prosperity at home and abroad, leading members such as philosopher and scientist John Desaguliers founded the Grand Lodge of England in London on June 24, 1717. This date marks the beginning of modern Masonry as a hierarchically structured organization devoted to the spread of the highest religious ideals through symbolism and ritual.

By that time, Masonic thinking and practices had already reached the shores of the New World. Masonry had been brought to North America by early colonists, government administrators and military personnel. The first officially constituted Masonic lodges in the Americas were organized by government-appointee and first American grand master Henry Price in Boston in 1731; in Norfolk, Virginia, two years later; and in Philadelphia in 1734 by Benjamin Franklin. As mentioned earlier, the first Masonic Lodge in Nova Scotia warranted by the Grand Lodge of England was set up in Annapolis Royal in 1739 by Erasmus James Philipps, the nephew of the former governor. The second lodge was created in Halifax in the same year of its founding, by Governor Edward Cornwallis in 1749. However, Masonic historians acknowledge that the Fraternity gathered and was active the continent for several years before the establishment of officially sanctioned lodges. In fact, it is quite likely that Masonry and Rosicrucianism were present in the very first colonial settlements at Jamestown and Port-Royal.

Of course, the origins of Masonry reach much further back in time. Little material on Masonic matters was publically available until 1898, when the multi-volumed *History of Freemasonry* appeared. Published by the Masonic Publishing Company of New York, it contained the extensive and detailed writings of two of Masonry's most respected historians, William Singleton and Albert Mackey, both of whom had entered into the thirty-third degree, the highest initiation level attainable among Masons.

Published in the wake of accusations of serious wrongdoings and North American condemnation of its secretive and therefore highly suspicious activities, this book sought to quiet the waves of criticism and fear-mongering. By providing page after page of exhaustive detail on the various aspects and activities of the Order, it sought to "lay before the public a correct and rational account of the nature, origin and progress of the institution."

Singleton, in a chapter called "Legends and Symbols of Masonry," provided a succinct if obtuse definition of the Fraternity's essential nature, which he said is "the Science of Morality, veiled in Allegory and illustrated by Symbols." Fortunately for the uninitiated, he took the trouble to elaborate:

> Of the various modes of communicating instruction to the uninformed, the Masonic student is particularly interested in two; namely, the instruction by legends and by symbols. It is to these two, almost exclusively, that he is indebted for all that he knows, and for all that he can know, of the philosophic system which is taught in the institution. . . . The Freemason has no way of reaching any of the esoteric teachings of the Order except through the medium of a legend or symbol. . . . Such are the legends (and symbols) in the Masonic degrees. . . . Hence we arrive at the truthfulness of the allegorical system, which was originally to teach the morality contained in the Institution.

Singleton went on to clarify the inner meanings of the symbolism and ritual utilized by Masonry, and the Order's ultimate goal:

> In these we recognize the several duties incumbent upon all men, which were inculcated in every system of morality taught by the ancient patriarchs and philosophers, our duty to God, our duty to ourselves, and our duty to all men. In these are found the realisms of Masonry, and not in our legends and allegories, by which they are veiled and concealed. The science of symbolism is perhaps as old as any other science. The learning of the ancient world was originally conveyed by symbolism. Freemasonry continues the ancient method as the best means of imparting its moral lessons, by *symbols*, which word, derived from the Greek, means to compare one thing to another. . . . The

Masonic symbolism, the private language of the craft

legend is a spoken symbol and is employed in Masonic teaching. . . . It is the language of poetry, in some countries (the legend) is an acted drama, in others it is merely recited or read; in both, it is designed to convey to the mind important moral truths. . . . Masonry's fundamental principle is a belief in God, without which there can be neither morality or philosophy. . . . Liberty, peace and tranquillity are the only objects worthy of Masons' diligence and trouble.

A perceptive examination of history shows that many of the leading artistic, intellectual, religious and political personalities upon the world stage have been interested in understanding the sacred mysteries. Secret schools of ancient knowledge were present throughout history in almost every land, and sometimes they grew up within established institutions of the day. Sometimes out of fear of persecution by the suspicious orthodoxy or intolerant ruler of the day, these schools went underground and their existence and whereabouts were known to only a few. These schools sought to instruct their students in the laws of the universe and bring about personal transformation for the benefit of themselves and others. The legends and cryptology associated with Freemasonry for hundreds of years and still in use today show that it originated out of such traditions.

Masonic historians hold divergent theories concerning the origins of the Order's philosophy, but all agree it originated in antiquity. Although they may differ as to the precise time and place of its progenesis, the theories most commonly propounded are often complimentary and enable one to retrace the earliest plausible beginnings of the Fraternity's teachings.

Masonic author Dr. L. Weisse stated that "Masonry began with Creation." Edward Spratt, a Masonic writer living in the mid-1800s, claimed that Adam was the first Mason, who "even after his expulsion from paradise retained great knowledge, especially in geometry." However, the majority of claims fall short of such definitive beginnings.

Many Masonic historians refer to early Israel and the building of King Solomon's Temple as the time and place where the teachings of their Craft were first exercised. Others identify with ancient Egypt and the construction of the Great Pyramid, and still others trace the Fraternity's origin to the Jewish religious sect of the Essenes. Some Masons view the great Roman architect Vitruvius as the originator of the Craft, and the Greek mystic and mathematician Pythagoras also figures prominently in some of the early histories of Masonry.

However, common philosophical and mystical threads connect these different schools of thought and their separate points of historical origin. In the revived Masonic movement of the sixteenth century, these divergent streams were formulated into a unified body of teachings within a framework of mystical Christianity. The renowned English-born Masonic writers William Hutchinson and George Oliver, who wrote in the late eighteenth and early nineteenth centuries, both emphasized the inherently Christian nature of the symbols at the centre of Masonic teaching. For them, Christ personified the Grand Architect of the Universe, the central figure of Masonry.

Belief in the existence of God is the fundamental basis of all modern Freemasonry, so essential that the Order has a rule that no self-proclaimed atheist can become a Mason. The new member is required to profess belief in God as part of preparation for initiation. The historian Hutchinson says the worship of God "was the first and corner-stone on which our originals thought it expedient to place the foundation of Masonry." The religion Masonry espouses is universal, and a required belief in God is not believed by Masons to contradict this universality. "Be assured" says Masonic author Godfrey Higgins "that God is equally present with the pious Hindu in the temple, the Jew in the synagogue, the Mohammedan in the Mosque and the Christian in the church."

At the time of Jesus' appearance in Palestine, three religious sects were present in Judea—the Pharisees, the Sadducees and the Essenes—and every Jew was expected to belong to one of them. The Jewish historian Flavius Josephus, in his *Antiquities of the Jews*, wrote about the Essenes with great admiration of their piety, unwavering commitment to the teachings of the Jewish prophets and knowledge of prediction and dream interpretation. Living in remote desert hilltop communities, its members followed a stricter lifestyle than the other two religious sects. Like similar groups in the Middle East at the time, they believed in reincarnation and the impending arrival of the Jewish Messiah.

Many Biblical researchers and writers now believe that Jesus and John the Baptist were reared and educated as Essenes. Interpretations of material from the Dead Sea also indicate that many of their precepts and prophecies were later given expression and fulfilled by Jesus himself.

Masonic historians such as William Lawrie and Christian Ginsburg not only draw comparisons between their fraternity and the Essenes but place Jesus as the bridge between the two. Certainly the early Christian communities were similar to those of the Essenes in some respects.

The life and teachings of Jesus led to the creation of the first-century esoteric Christian sect known as the Gnostics. Many Biblical scholars believe Gnosticism had its roots not only in the teachings of Jesus but also in the Jewish Essenic mystical tradition. Both the Essenes and the Gnostics, like Jesus, were conversant with the profound use of symbolism and allegory and with the prophetic tradition.

Deriving its name from the Greek word *gnosis*, meaning knowledge, Gnosticism advocated, as Jesus had done, an inner and more direct relationship with God. It also sought to integrate the teachings of the ancient school of philosophy at Alexandria in Egypt, the Jewish secret doctrine known as Cabalism and the mystical doctrines of Asia with the simpler and more personal teachings of the new religion of the Nazarene, given the name Christianity by the Greeks at Antioch. Gnosticism in turn led to the formation of later esoteric Christian sects such as the medieval Cathars of southern France and also exerted an influence upon the religious thinking of the Knights Templar, who encountered it during their sojourn in Jerusalem during the time of the Crusades. Transplanted to Europe, it formed the basis for teachings found in present-day Masonry and Rosicrucianism.

Of particular relevence to the Oak Island mystery is the importance of the figure Hermes to Masons. In Albert Mackey's monumental work, *Encyclopaedia of Freemasonry and its Kindred Sciences*, published in 1875, Hermes is said to be the Founder of Masonry. In the "Grand Lodge Manuscript," dated 1632, it is said—and the statement is substantially the same in all earlier writings—that "The great Hermarines that was Cubys sonne, the which Cuby was Semmes son, that was Noah's sonne. This same Hermarines was afterwards called Hermes the father of Wisdom; he found one of the two pillars of stone, and found the science written thereon, and he taught it to other men."

Drawing from a smorgasbord of sources of sacred history, including Greek, Roman, Hebraic and early Christian, Mackey adds that this Hermes was the inventor of Egyptian hieroglyphics and a renowned philosopher who wrote more than thirty books, including some on medicine, all of which have been lost. This same Hermes was also claimed by the medieval alchemists to be the founder of their art, which they called the Hermetic science and from which are derived the Hermetic Rites and Hermetic Degrees present in Masonry.

In the first ages of the Christian Church, this legendary Egyptian philosopher was in fact considered the inventor of everything known to the human intellect. It was said that Pythagoras and Plato had both derived their knowledge from him, and that he had recorded his inventions on pillars.

In a more contemporary publication entitled *The First Freemasons*, a detailed study of Masonry in Scotland, David Stevenson reaffirms the Masons' traditional philosophical connection with Hermes and ancient Egypt in his reference to the re-emergence of the Hermetic movement during the years of the European Renaissance and its influence on the evolution of the sixteenth-century Masonic movement in Scotland through William Schaw, considered one of the architects of modern Masonry. Stevenson states:

> Closely bound up with the search for wisdom through astrology and alchemy, Hermeticism assumed that as ancient Egypt predated the civilisations of Greece and Rome, its lost knowledge must be more valuable and pure. The movement got its name from the mythical figure of Hermes Trismegistes. The writing attributed to this supposed Egyptian sage in fact dated from the early Christian era, but they were believed to be many centuries older. Through study of these works and of ancient Egypt (especially of the hieroglyphics in which the Egyptians were supposed to have concealed their wisdom from the eyes of the profane) men hoped to unlock the mysteries of the distant past. But the search was not simply historical and scientific.
>
> In its essence it was a spiritual quest, and so purification and spiritual enlightenment were essential to success—as, many believed, was secrecy, for the great mysteries were the preserve of the dedicated initiate. In the light of Hermetic ideas the mediaeval myths of the Masons take on a new importance. The myths claimed that the craft had its roots in ancient Egypt; and the Old

Charges (writings) specifically assigned Hermes Trismegistes an important role in the pro-cess. In the generations in which the great Hermetic quest swept across Europe, Masons must have taken a particular pride in the role of the god-like Hermes in their craft histories, and considering the extent of the obsession it is not implausible to think of William Schaw as seeing one aspect of the secret lodges he created as being a grafting of the ambitions that led to the founding of secret Hermetic societies onto a craft which already claimed that it had a connection with Hermes and that some of its wisdom derived from ancient Egypt.

In this light, the core of ritual which lay at the heart of the new lodges can be seen as involving them in some sense in the Hermetic quest. The idea of Schaw believing Scottish stonemasons had a part to play in recovering lost ancient wisdom essential to the future of mankind may seem absurd in cold blood; in the highly charged atmosphere of 1600 in which many felt all stability and certainty was collapsing it becomes plausible.

This tradition of Hermes as the father of Freemasonry not only gives the Fraternity an extremely ancient origin but identifies architecture, mathematics and symbolism as of spiritual significance within the Masonic mindset from earliest times. Again, in Masonic lore, Hermes is looked upon as the originator of hieroglyphics, and the process of acquiring Masonic degrees incorporates this traditional knowledge. Of chief importance to the committed Mason, of course, is the inner transformational process initiated by the rituals and their symbolism; identification of Hermes as the father of Masonry has more to do with his benevolent God-like consciousness than with the fact that he was an architect.

Interestingly, some Jewish scholars consider Hermes and the Biblical patriarch Enoch to be one and the same. Enoch, who "walked with God," is said to have taught with great wisdom and to have constructed a temple and an underground vault for the preservation of his teachings and religious treasures, including a bejewelled equilateral triangle made of gold, prior to the Great Flood. Certain Masonic scholars also revere Enoch and credit him as the inventor of writing, the art of building and the Craft of Masonry. The psychic Edgar Cayce referred to Hermes as the builder of the Great Pyramid at Giza following the inundation of Atlantis, records of which, according to Cayce, were deposited in a Hermetically sealed chamber deep underground near the Sphinx.

Another important story concerning the ancient origins of Masonry is drawn from the Biblical story of the building of King Solomon's Temple in Jerusalem, which occurred about 1000 B.C. The craft of architecture and the use of secret signs are also key components of this legend, while the central character is the master builder Hiram Abif. The events surrounding Abif's death at the hands of three of his workers have become part of the highly ritual-istic initiation into the third degree, that of a Master Mason. In the modern re-enactment of this tale the initiate is symbolically raised from the dead, in harmony with the Christian theme of spiritual renewal and resurrection at the core of Masonic teaching.

In one version of the story, Hiram is said to have worn a golden triangle, engraved with the Master's word, around his neck. After Hiram's death, King Solomon had this triangle placed on a triangu-lar altar in a secret vault built under the most remote part of the Temple. The triangle was further concealed by a cubical stone on which the sacred law had been described. The vault, known only to the twenty-seven elect, was then walled up. Three of the symbols mentioned here—the triangle, the vault and the inscribed stone—reoccur throughout the history of Freemasonry. In fact, the initiation ritual within Masonry known as the Cryptic Rite Degree has as its central focus the discovery of the sacred secret within a buried vault. Thus ritualistic burial and rediscovery of sacred treasure is very much part of Masonic lore.

From all of the above it is obvious that Masonry draws its sym-bolism and rituals from a rich cultural mosaic and an ancient unify-ing faith. The craft, tools, closed organizational structure and secret codes used by medieval stonemasons were adopted by sixteenth-century students of occult wisdom as a convenient way to pass on mystical teachings while protecting themselves from unnecessary ridicule and the threat of state and Church persecution.

Although Masonry survived witch hunts from various quarters and eventually gained a measure of recognition as a legitimate religious organization, it retained its traditions of ritualistic initiation, secrecy and cryptic symbolism and these were transferred to North America during the early days of the English, French and Scottish colonies.

Several symbols associated with Masonry's origins are evident in the hieroglyphics and stone markings found on Oak Island. The sealed Pit, its unusual materials and the buried vault hint that ritual was involved in the creation of the mystery, and it may be that only those with an appreciation of Masonic ritual will be able to solve it.

21

Psychic Insights

During the past two hundred years many psychics have been consulted about the Oak Island mystery, and many people have had psychic experiences of one kind or another while associated with the treasure search.

Psychic ability, like that exercised by proven and reputable practitioners such as Edgar Cayce, is basically a focused and beneficial use of mental faculties not normally available to the conscious mind. Through various processes, most genuine psychics, people with an ability to consciously tune into the subconscious or superconscious levels of mind, endeavour to provide clearer insight or suggest solutions to problems of various kinds, from personal health and relationships to business and career to national and world events.

Psychic ability has been used under various guises since the beginning of time and in all cultures by individuals exceptionally gifted or especially trained for the purpose. It is mentioned many times in the Bible and in the written histories of all world religions. It is recognized in psychology as a legitimate if rather unpredictable function of mind. As has been well documented by the media, psychic ability, whether we understand it or not, can be of immense help in dealing with the everyday opportunities and challenges of life.

Psychic abilities are by no means the quirky pursuit of the mentally fragile or emotionally frustrated. Hard-nosed police agencies and no-nonsense business executives have been known to consult with psychics. Some members of the medical profession have adopted a receptive attitude to the potential use of psychic ability as an alternative diagnostic and therapeutic tool, and in recent years psychics have been consulted on some archaeological digs.

Of course, as is the case in every profession, there are good and bad psychics and some are genuine and some are charlatans.

Psychic ability is not exclusive to people who call themselves psychics. We all experience psychic ability in one form or another from time to time. Sometimes it manifests in the form of a dream, a vision, a premonition or just an intuitive hunch. We may find our-selves thinking of someone, and the next moment we pick up a ring-ing telephone to find them on the other end of the line. We can all learn, as Cayce, Rudolf Steiner and others have pointed out, to develop our psychic abilities by natural means.

The mining industry has long valued the profit-producing work of mineral dowsers, individuals who can, with the help of metal rods, sense the location of minerals deep underground. On Oak Island, Dan Blankenship has used dowsing, once the sole province of water diviners, to confirm the locations of known caverns and tunnels.

Many key figures in the Oak Island treasure search have consult-ed psychics over the years. Both Frederick Blair and Melbourne Chappell attended an automatic writing session conducted by psy-chic John Wicks of Saginaw, Michigan, in 1931. Wicks became a channel for a spirit who claimed he was a Spanish priest who had lived in South America at the time of the Incas. This disincarnate spirit then provided a detailed account of little-known aspects of Oak Island and what he claimed was the source of the Oak Island treasure. Blair and Chappell were quite impressed by the routine and the information, but Wicks' promised financial involvement did not materialize because in a later session his spirit guide allegedly warned him the time was not yet right for the Oak Island treasure to be discovered.

Laverne Johnson, who did some exploring on the island in the early 1960s, consulted with Madame Fontaine, a well-known West Coast clairvoyant, on three different occasions. During the first visit she used Tarot cards and gave him a reading which indicated in some detail that something important was buried adjacent to the swamp in the centre of the island. During a later visit she provided him with different information that compared favourably with his own conclusions about the location of the treasure. On this occasion she was possibly picking up this information from Johnson's sub-conscious. Johnson eventually ran out of time and money and could not prove or disprove his theory.

In 1976 a husband and wife psychic team from Texas spent a number of weeks on the island. They claimed they experienced psy-chic visions of a vast religious treasure concealed in a huge cavern underneath the centre of the island which can be accessed by tunnels leading to it from the swamp. They also said dead bodies would be found in the depths of the island, and that the treasure contained a collection of manuscripts, including a blue-covered book with a cross on its cover. Both husband and wife claimed they saw a multitude of religious artifacts, some of which were up to three thousand years old. They concluded that the treasure was hidden on Oak Island for a spiritual purpose, and that it would only be retrieved when the motives of those searching on the island were more altruistic.

Writer D'Arcy O'Connor contacted Boston-based psychic Eugenia Macer-Story while working on his first book about Oak Island. Using a small pendulum suspended by hand over a map of the island, she located several points of primary and secondary importance to the treasure search. These she later confirmed by placing her hand on the same map and, with her eyes closed, feeling a noticeable heat increase in her palm at the appropriate points. Some of her strong responses were over the swamp area.

My own research and experience of the beneficial use of psychic ability naturally had made me curious about its applicability at Oak Island. As described earier, I myself had experienced a dream about a treasure location within a day of arriving at Oak Island.

I also invited Terry Murphy, one of Nova Scotia's most respected psychics, to talk at the October 1993 Oak Island Conference. On the Friday afternoon, while we were on the island as part of a live broadcast of the "Live at Five" television news magazine program, she wandered off alone in the hope of tuning into some aspect of the island's secret. At one point she returned to ask me if any other people were on the island besides ourselves, the television crew and the Blankenships. After checking and assuring her there were not, she told me she had "seen" men in colourful clothing in among the trees on the hilltop at the eastern end of the island. I returned to the site with her but saw no-one. Terry then walked down by the shoreline at Smith's Cove before returning to the Pit area to participate in an interview. After we had completed our segment of the fast-paced show, we returned to a nearby hotel.

On the way, Terry told me she had not discussed all of her psychic impressions during her brief television interview. In the company of another friend back at the hotel, she described a vision she had had of a large group of men in cross-emblazoned robes coming ashore on the island. She said she was aware that they belonged to a much earlier time and were involved in the final stages of concealing a treasure on the island. She had also noticed they were carrying ashore a large leather-bound box, which she sensed was the final and perhaps most important part of the treasure. Once on shore, they proceeded in a procession to a point further inland. Terry sensed this group was completing an important task that had been entrusted to it.

On Saturday evening, after she had finished the formal part of her presentation on psychic ability and its possible use as an aid to archaeology, I asked her to talk about her unusual insights of the previous day. Her account of the procession ashore of the men in robes brought an immediate, surprised response from Helène Thibert, a woman who had helped arrange the conference. She excitedly disclosed that she had experienced a dream with similar content some weeks earlier. Later that evening, Terry identified in a book on display at the conference the style of cross she had seen on the robes worn by the men carrying the treasure box ashore. It was the characteristic eight-pointed cross of the twelfth-century order of the Knights Templar of Jerusalem. This same emblem has appeared on ceremonial clothing worn in Masonic ritual for centuries.

Over the years I have had several dreams and experiences of a psychic nature; as has been repeatedly documented, we can all be psychic through the medium of dreams. In view of my intense interest in the Oak Island mystery, my inability during the early months of my research to visit the island, and the apparent lack of interest on the part of those directly involved in discussing any theories about the treasure itself, I decided to incubate a dream about Oak Island, hoping to receive some insight into what the mystery was all about.

Dream incubation is a process whereby one induces a dream about a given subject to acquire information not available to the conscious mind. It requires preparations on the dreamer's part, such as writing down the issue or problem to be dreamt about and a straightforward question needing resolution. I had previously applied the process with some success and felt certain it could help me in my research. I sat at my desk, wrote down some relevant details about Oak Island and phrased a question about the nature of the treasure. The resulting dramatic dream was much more than I had expected and had a profound effect on my attitude towards the Oak Island mystery.

In the dream I found myself once again on Oak Island, this time in a loosely wooded area of tall trees. It was bright daylight and my attention was immediately drawn to the ground around me, which was a rich luminous green. The moss-covered soil radiated an energy which seemed to come from an underground source. I was immensely awed by the scene. Then, as I proceeded to walk forward, I noticed powerful shafts of sunlight beginning to stream down into the glade. Again I was struck by the vibrant quality of this light and felt exhilarated. I sensed something phenomenal was about to happen. Suddenly I was totally aware that the real value of the treasure hidden on the island lay in its connection to Christ. I turned quickly to share this exciting information and found two women I recognized standing on either side of me. I was breathless with excitement as I shared this remarkable revelation with them.

I woke from this dream in a state of elation and its highly charged emotional and visual contents remained with me for several days. It confirmed for me, more than anything I had read to that point, that the real value of the Oak Island treasure lay in its universal spiritual significance. My later discoveries of Masonic and Rosicrucian connections to the island and its treasure only served to bolster the legitimacy of this insight.

22

Conclusions

On the basis of the extensive man-made workings already found on Oak Island, including the highly effective water-trap system; the many cryptically marked stones; the large symbolic stone markers; drilling samples from the Pit area and elsewhere; radiocarbon dating; and convincing images on videotape and in photographs of the 230-foot-deep cavern, one is left with no alternative but to conclude that a major project involving the concealment of something of great value took place on Oak Island between 300 and 450 years ago.

From what has been revealed on the island to date, it is obvious that individuals with expert knowledge of navigation, mining and marine engineering planned and supervised this project. It is also clearly evident that a well-organized, disciplined body of men were engaged in the work over a period of many months and possibly years, and the operation must have been well financed.

One is led to the conclusion that a very powerful motivation lay behind the project.

The whole operation was carried out in strict secrecy and that secrecy has been maintained to this day.

There is repeated evidence of a Masonic/Rosicrucian connection to and interest in the mystery. The symbols found on the island indicate that the group who buried the treasure and possibly some aspect of the treasure itself were of an esoteric Christian nature.

Historical research points to the strong possibility that Sir Francis Bacon or some of his close associates was or were connected to the undertaking.

Psychic insights have confirmed that something of significant spiritual value has been elaborately concealed on Oak Island.

I share the conclusion arrived at by others before me that Oak Island was used in part as the repository for a sacred treasure, and I strongly believe that if it is ever to be physically retrieved, and further dangers, frustrations and escalating costs avoided, then the attitude towards the treasure search must change.

I believe a very different approach is required to safely recover the treasure. The approach needs to be much more comprehensive, combining psychic ability and archaeology, an understanding of cryptographics and symbolism, sophisticated exploration technology and state-of-the-art excavation equipment. I hope that one day soon an easily accessible entrance into the elaborate underground workings will be found, so the flooding system can be cut off or diverted and the well-protected treasure can at last be retrieved. Like many others, I am concerned that the crude measures employed by previous treasure hunters may have already destroyed or damaged much of the treasure and its possibly valuable manuscripts.

The licensing of the Oak Island treasure search goes back to the middle of the nineteenth century, when the first license was issued on behalf of the British Crown. In the mid-1950s the Nova Scotia legislature, at the instigation of Frederick Blair and Mel Chappell, passed a special Treasure Trove license amendment specifically dealing with buried treasure. This measure even allowed a treasure hunter to encroach and dig on property owned by another party, as was done on Oak Island at the time. In return, the province was to receive ten per cent of any treasure found, but the reporting of any discovery was left up to the discretion and honesty of the treasure hunter.

Then in 1989 the Nova Scotia government of the day passed legislation requiring future treasure hunters to also apply for a heritage research permit or a letter of exemption. Issued by the curator of special places for the province, this permit required treasure hunters to adhere to more stringent controls and regulations and was intended to prevent further destruction of artifacts or sites of archaeological or historical significance. However, in spite of the interesting discoveries made on Oak Island over the years, the site was exempted from this permit and has remained so ever since. According to the government officials I consulted, no detailed archaeological survey has ever been carried out on the island.

In reply to several questions on this issue, Don Downe, the province's minister of natural resources, stated that although it is regrettable that better care was not taken of Oak Island in the past, controls now in place ensure that little additional damage will be done. However, when I asked to view documentation of any assessment of Oak Island carried out under the Special Places Act, Downe replied that such documentation was confidential.

Although the Oak Island Exploration Company has stated it will have an archaeologist on site in the event of a major excavation, it is actually not bound by the research regulations under the heritage permit legislation.

Following the 1993 Oak Island Conference, a petition calling for a government-sponsored archaeological program on the island was submitted to the provincial and federal governments. Their replies indicated that the petition would be kept on file to be considered when existing licenses were up for renewal. As of 1995, the Oak Island Exploration Company had applied for an early renewal of its five-year license.

Given that someone as experienced and qualified as Mendel Peterson of the Smithsonian Institution has stated that Oak Island is a fascinating archaeological site with the potential to be of great historical significance, a view now shared by many others, it is to be hoped that the Nova Scotia and Canadian governments will show some interest in this aspect of the mystery.

In view of the discoveries already made on Oak Island and the importance of other archaeological and treasure sites world-wide, it is surely time that a detailed archaeological survey was undertaken on the island. The importance to humankind of contemporary discoveries of artifacts in Egypt and the Yucatan, and the discovery of the Dead Sea Scrolls in Israel should encourage us to undertake such a project.

This survey need not hinder the ongoing search for the treasure. In fact, it might even attract additional private investors to the project, which, as David Tobias knows only too well, needs and deserves all the support it can get.

The recovery of the treasure will not only end one of the longest treasure hunts in history; more importantly, it could throw light on a highly significant event in our past that can be of relevance to us today. Of course, the physical recovery of the treasure may only be the first stage in understanding the full significance of the Oak Island mystery. But I am certain that, as Reginald Harris, the former Grand Master of Nova Scotia Masons, wrote, "there is a lot more to the true story of Oak Island and some day it will be told in full."

Epilogue

During 1996 several developments occurred in the Oak Island treasure search. Early in the year, Oak Island Discoveries Inc., financed by Boston millionaire David Mugar, withdrew from the treasure hunt, partly because of the rift that developed between David Tobias and Dan Blankenship over the nature of Mugar's involvement. The results of the ground and sea investigative work carried out by the Woods Hole Oceanographic Research Institute on behalf of the company were not released. Possibly, they were not encouraging, although Tobias was reported in the local press as saying that an important discovery might soon be announced. Few Oak Island observers held their breath, having heard similar comments several times before.

Shortly after Blankenship's 12 exploration licenses expired in early July, the Nova Scotia Department of Natural Resources issued the garrulous Gary Clayton, a seasonal treasure hunter, his third two-year license, permitting him to dig for treasure on Little Mash (Plumb) Island, located just west of the causeway. Meanwhile, New Brunswicker Ladislav Molnar, having repeatedly had his application to explore for pirate treasure on the larger Frog Island turned down, made it known that he was petitioning Queen Elizabeth II to intervene on his behalf, on the basis that the Queen's law ruled in Canada. However, as exploration rights on this island were already covered by the license held by Oak Island Explorations Ltd., this appeal to Buckingham Palace was in vain. The disappointed Molnar was advised by provincial officials to apply again prior to the expiry of the existing license, at the end of the year.

At the same time, Dan Blankenship attempted to obtain a license, on behalf of the newly formed Mahone Bay Exploration Company Ltd., for lot 23 on Oak Island, the site on which he built his house over 20 years ago. Then, surprisingly, Oak Island Explorations Ltd., which has held the license under different names for most of Oak Island for the past 30 years, was refused an early renewal of its five-year permit, which expired December 31, 1996.

The outcome of all this was that the indomitable Fred Nolan became the only legally authorised treasure hunter on the island at the start of 1997. His existing license was to expire in May 1998. Having earlier sold his lot 5 on the north west end of the island to woodworker Robert Young, in an arrangement that also involved Young in the treasure search, Fred spent part of 1996 retracing his investigative steps on his 24-acre centre island property. Still energetic and active, he moved the portable drilling rig close to the intersection of the cross and found some coconut fibre near the swamp.

During a recent meeting beside his museum by the causeway, we chatted about several matters including, once again, my dream of treasure being hidden in the treed area beside the swamp. As we parted company, Fred casually assured me, "We are making progress." Then, echoing a comment made to me earlier by his longtime competitor, he added, "But we need a little luck." Knowing what both he and Dan have been through in the last 30 years, I found myself hoping that both men get it, in spades.

Undoubtedly the most interesting development in 1996 was the underwater exploration around Oak Island conducted by the Canadian Hydrographic Service based at the Bedford Institute of Oceanography. On board the research vessel the *Plover* was some leading-edge technology for ocean floor exploration — the EM 3000 multibeam sonar survey mapping system. This vertical echo sounding device sends down an expanding pulse beam to the seabed that records its configurations as if the water was non-existent. While the vessel manoeuvred slowly in the channel between the mainland and the southeast shore of Oak Island, readings relayed back to the equipment on board suggested that a large hole and several mounds existed in South Shore Cove. Then, during the vessel's many grid-like passes off Smith's Cove, the equipment picked up data that indicated an extensive underwater wall, or berm, juts out at least 100 metres into the ocean from the east end of the island. A large depression was also located in Joudrey's Cove, off the island's north shore. According to geologist Gordon Fader and geophysicist Robert Courtney, of the Bedford Institute, the wall or berm is almost certainly a man-made construction, the finding of which presents a whole new set of questions about the Oak Island mystery.

Bibliography

Arpat, Atilla. "Secret Numerology and Geometry in the Churches of Nova Scotia." *Nova Scotia Historical Review* 14, no.1, June 1994.

Bacon, Delia. *The Philosophy of the Plays of Shakespeare Unfolded.* New York: AMS Press, 1970.

Bacon, Francis. *The Advancement of Learning and New Atlantis.* Richard Jones, ed. New York: Odyssey Press, 1937.

Baigent, Michael, and Richard Leigh. *The Temple and the Lodge.* London: Jonathan Cape, 1989.

Bayley, Harold. *The Tragedy of Sir Francis Bacon.* London: Grant Richards, 1902.

Bell, Winthrop P. *The Foreign Protestants and the Settlement of Nova Scotia.* Toronto: University of Toronto Press, 1961.

Bokenham, T.D. *The Baconiana Magazine.* Surrey, England, 1993.

Cayce, Edgar Evans. *Edgar Cayce on Atlantis.* New York: Warner Books, 1968.

Creighton, Helen. *Bluenose Ghosts.* Toronto: McGraw-Hill Ryerson, 1957.

Creighton, Helen. *Folklore of Lunenburg County, Nova Scotia.* Toronto: McGraw-Hill Ryerson, 1976.

Crooker, William S. *Oak Island Gold.* Halifax: Nimbus, 1993.

DesBrisay, Mather B. *History of the County of Lunenburg.* Toronto: William Briggs, 1895.

Dictionary of National Biography. Oxford: Oxford University Press.

Donnelly, Ignatius. Atlantis: *The Antediluvian World.* New York: Rudolf Steiner Publications, 1971.

Durant, Will and Ariel. *The Story of Civilization.* Volume VII. New York: Simon and Schuster, 1961.

Fitzgerald, Paula. *"I, Prince Tudor, Wrote Shakespeare."* Norfolk, Va: Corinthian, 1979.

Furneaux, Rupert. *The Money Pit Mystery.* New York: Dodd, Mead and Co., 1972.

Griffiths, Naomi. *The Acadians: Creation of a People.* Toronto: McGraw-Hill Ryerson, 1973.

Harris, Reginald V. *A Short History of Freemasonry in Nova Scotia.* Halifax: Grand Lodge of Nova Scotia, 1966.

Harris, Reginald V. *The Oak Island Mystery.* Toronto: McGraw-Hill Ryerson, 1958.

Heckethorn, Charles. *The Secret Societies of All Ages and Countries.* New York: University Books, 1965.

Insh, G.P. "Sir William Alexander's Colony at Port Royal." *The Dalhousie Review*, January 1930, Halifax.

Johnson, Laverne. *Revealed: The Secret of Oak Island.* Vancouver: Laverne Johnson, 1991.

Jones, Elizabeth. *Gentlemen and Jesuits*. Toronto: University of Toronto, 1986.

Jung, Carl G. *Man and His Symbols*. New York: Doubleday and Co., 1964.

Kaulback, Ruth E. *The Historic Saga of La Have.* Bridgewater, N.S.: Ruth E. Kaulback, 1970.

Leary, Thomas B. *The Oak Island Enigma.* Omaha, Neb.: Thomas B. Leary, 1953.

Levi, Eliphas. *The Mystery of the Qabalah.* Wellingborough, England.: Aquarian Press, 1981.

Lunn, Janet, and Christopher Moore. *The Story of Canada.* Toronto: Webster, 1992.

Mackey, Albert G. *The Encyclopedia of Freemasonry and Its Kindred Sciences.* Philadelphia: Moss and Co., 1875.

Mackey, Albert G. T*he History of Freemasonry.* New York: Masonic History Company, 1898.

McCreath, Peter, and John G. Leefe. *The History of Early Nova Scotia.* Tantallon N.S.: Four East, 1982.

McInnis, Edgar. *The North American Nations.* Toronto: J.M. Dent and Sons, 1963.

O'Connor, D'Arcy. *The Big Dig.* New York: Ballantine Books, 1988.

Raddall, Thomas H. Halifax: *Warden of the North.* Toronto: McClelland and Stewart, 1948.

Sharp, Rosiland. *Samuel de Champlain.* London: Fitzhenry, 1981.

Sinclair, Andrew. *The Sword and the Grail.* New York: Crown, 1992.

Singleton, William R. *The History of the Symbols of Freemasonry.* New York: Masonic History Company, 1898.

Smith, Mary Baldwin. *The Elizabethan World.* Boston: Houghton Mifflin, 1967.

Spedon, Andrew L. *Rambles among the Bluenoses.* Montreal: John Lovell, 1863.

Stevenson, David. *The First Freemasons.* Aberdeen, Scotland: Aberdeen University Press, 1988.

Sugrue, Thomas. *There is a River.* New York: Holt, Rinehart and Winston, 1942.

Young, George. *Ancient Peoples and Modern Ghosts.* Queensland, N.S.: George Young, 1980.